The CS Detective

THE CS
DETECTIVE

An Algorithmic Tale of Crime, Conspiracy, and Computation

jeremy kubica

SAN FRANCISCO

THE CS DETECTIVE. Copyright © 2016 by Jeremy Kubica.

Printed in USA

First printing

20 19 18 17 16   1 2 3 4 5 6 7 8 9

ISBN-10: 1-59327-749-0
ISBN-13: 978-1-59327-749-9

MIX
Paper from responsible sources
FSC
www.fsc.org
FSC® C014174

Publisher: William Pollock
Production Editor: Riley Hoffman
Cover and Interior Design: Beth Middleworth
Illustrator: Miran Lipovača
Developmental Editor: Liz Chadwick
Technical Reviewer: Heidi Newton
Copyeditor: Rachel Monaghan
Compositor: Riley Hoffman
Proofreader: Paula L. Fleming

For information on distribution, translations, or bulk sales, please contact No Starch Press, Inc. directly:

No Starch Press, Inc.
245 8th Street, San Francisco, CA 94103
phone: 415.863.9900; info@nostarch.com
www.nostarch.com

Library of Congress Cataloging-in-Publication Data
Names: Kubica, Jeremy.
Title: The CS detective : an algorithmic tale of crime, conspiracy, and
    computation / by Jeremy Kubica.
Description: San Francisco : No Starch Press, [2016] | Summary: "A mystery
    novel for computer science students and enthusiasts that introduces the
    concepts behind search algorithms and data structures. Each chapter
    teaches a new concept, ending with a technical explanation."-- Provided by
    publisher.
Identifiers: LCCN 2016013632 (print) | LCCN 2016026435 (ebook) | ISBN
    9781593277499 (pbk.) | ISBN 1593277490 (pbk.) | ISBN 9781593277871 (epub)
    | ISBN 1593277873 (epub) | ISBN 9781593277888 (mobi) | ISBN 1593277881
    (mobi)
Subjects: | CYAC: Algorithms--Fiction. | Computer science--Fiction. | Mystery
    and detective stories.
Classification: LCC PZ7.1.K8 Cs 2016 (print) | LCC PZ7.1.K8 (ebook) | DDC
    [Fic]--dc23
LC record available at https://lccn.loc.gov/2016013632

ABOUT THE AUTHOR

Jeremy Kubica is a principal engineer at Google working on machine learning and algorithms. He has a PhD in robotics from Carnegie Mellon University and a BS in computer science from Cornell University. He spent his graduate school years creating algorithms to detect killer asteroids (actually stopping them was, of course, left as "future work"). Kubica is the author of the popular *Computational Fairy Tales* blog.

ABOUT THE TECHNICAL REVIEWER

Heidi Newton has a BSc from the University of Canterbury, New Zealand, and an MSc from Victoria University of Wellington, New Zealand, both in computer science. She works for the University of Canterbury's computer science education research group and Code Avengers, and on the side carries out related tutoring and consultancy work. Her current focus is on improving teaching resources for computer science and programming.

CONTENTS

Acknowledgments

I am tremendously grateful to all the people who contributed to, worked on, and supported this book.

I would like to start by thanking the whole team at No Starch Press. In particular, I would like to thank Liz Chadwick and Riley Hoffman for their excellent help, guidance, and suggestions during the editing process. Liz's brilliant suggestions were invaluable for keeping the story focused and moving. I am also grateful for her ideas in shaping the lecture notes format of the technical sections. Thank you to Bill Pollock and Tyler Ortman for their support, and a special thanks to Bill for suggesting the title. I would also like to thank Carlos Bueno for pointing me to No Starch Press.

Thank you to Miran Lipovača for his amazing illustrations. They truly capture the characters and the story.

Thank you to Heidi Newton for her thorough and insightful technical review. Her work was vital in ensuring the concepts came across both accurately and understandably. I appreciate the number of times she warned of explanations being too technical and thus inaccessible to students.

A tremendous thanks goes out to all the people who slogged through earlier versions of this book and provided valuable feedback: John Bull, Mike Hochberg, Edith Kubica, Regan Lee, and Kristen "Kit" Stubbs, PhD. Thank you to Ilana Schwarcz, who edited the earlier version of the manuscript and helped smooth out many of the rough edges.

A deep thank you to my family for their support. In particular, thank you to my parents for supporting my interest in computer science as a kid and for providing significant encouragement for this book.

A Note to Readers

This book focuses on computational thinking and search algorithms. The stories introduce and illustrate computational concepts at a high level, exploring the motivation behind them and their application in a noncomputer domain. This book is not a comprehensive text, and the stories are not intended as a substitute for a solid technical description of computer science. Instead, they are meant to be used like illustrations: they supplement the full concept and aid understanding.

The book covers a variety of computational approaches that all share the broad categorization of *search algorithms*. Concepts are presented first within the context of the story, and then explained more technically in a section laid out as lecture notes at the end of each chapter. Readers can safely skip these technical sections without missing any of the story.

This book assumes some experience with basic computer science concepts but does not require knowledge of any specific programming language. The algorithms in this book are meant to apply to a range of programming languages and problem domains.

— 1 —
Search Problems

The door opened without a knock—only the hinge's creak announced the visitor. Frank started for his crossbow, but pulled up short. If the Vinettees were coming for him, they would have knocked—with an axe. Whoever was coming through the door must want to talk. Frank reached for his mug instead and downed the remainder of his now-cold coffee.

"Captain Donovan," he said as the man entered. "What brings you to this fine neighborhood? I thought you didn't venture below Fifteenth Street anymore."

"It's been a while," the captain said simply. "How've you been, Frank?"

"Spectacular," Frank answered dryly, eyeing the captain as he walked a slow circuit around the room.

Donovan scanned Frank's shabby office. His red officer's cloak swished gently behind him. "How's the private eye game?"

"It pays the bills," Frank lied.

The captain nodded. He paused for a moment, then moved to the bookshelf and browsed the contents.

"So is this a social visit then?" Frank said. "Should I be asking after Marlene and the kids?"

"They're quite well," replied Donovan without turning around. "Marlene's turtle-grooming business is doing well these days. Bill joined the force last year. And Veronica is an accountant, just about the last thing we would have—"

"I wasn't actually asking," Frank interrupted.

The captain shrugged. He pulled a book from the shelf and leafed through the pages. Frank craned his neck to see the cover—*Police Academy Yearbook: Class XXI.*

"What do you want, Captain?" Frank demanded.

The captain met Frank's stare at last. "I need your help, Frank," he said.

Frank straightened. In the five years since Frank had left the force, the captain had paid him exactly two visits, and both had been to warn him to stay away from active cases. Threats were all Frank had come to expect, but now it seemed the captain had a special kind of problem—perhaps the kind that would mean an end to Frank's delinquent rent.

"I'm not on the force anymore," said Frank airily. "Why don't you get one of your trusted detectives to do it?"

"I need someone outside of the force," said the captain. "Drop the act, Frank. If you don't know what it means for me to be here, you're not the person I need."

Frank chuckled. "A leak? On *your* force?"

"Worse. Last night someone broke into the station's record room and stole over 500 scrolls."

"What were they after?" asked Frank. Without thinking, he leaned forward in his chair and reached for a fresh scroll and a quill. The movement came automatically to him, like drinking coffee or avoiding stairs.

"I don't know," said Donovan. "There was no pattern. They stole whole shelves of documents, everything from property disputes to expense reports. They took all the ledgers we keep on assassins, celebrities, private investigators, notaries . . . They even took both boxes of Farmer Swinson's noise complaints. But other shelves were completely untouched. We counted at least 512 missing documents."

"Maybe it was one of Farmer Swinson's neighbors," joked Frank. "They must've heard that after a mere hundred complaints, an intern will come to your house and give you a stern lecture."

Captain Donovan didn't bother to reply. He just stared pityingly until Frank cleared his throat and broke the silence. "So you want me to find these documents?"

The captain shook his head. "I want you to find the thieves. We have backups of the documents. I want to know what information they needed and what they plan to do with it."

"A search problem," Frank mused. During his time on the force, his two specialties had been search problems and annoying the captain.

"Does the king know?" Frank asked.

"I briefed him yesterday," said the captain, a hint of annoyance in his voice. "Ever since the trouble with that crackpot wizard, the king insists on daily briefings on everything." Two years ago, a megalomaniac wizard named Exponentious had tried to destroy the entire kingdom. Since then King Fredrick had personally instituted sweeping upgrades to the kingdom's security, with over 300 new security regulations, at least 5 of which dealt with the storage of official documents in government buildings under 10 stories tall.

"I can't blame him though," Donovan grumbled. "It was a close call. If it hadn't been for Princess Ann, who knows where the kingdom would be now."

Frank nodded silently. Exponentious had attacked the algorithmic foundations of the kingdom by cursing the scholars who studied those algorithms. Within months he had rendered even simple operations inefficient, and the kingdom had started to grind to a halt. Evidence of the damage had been everywhere; even in his local bakery, Frank had himself witnessed panic break out as customers discovered they couldn't remember how to arrange themselves into a line.

"The king has, of course, taken a personal interest in the matter," the captain continued irritably. "He wants all the details: Who's assigned to the case? Which search algorithms are we using? Have we scoured all of the neighboring buildings?"

Frank stifled a chuckle and mulled over the proposition. A consulting gig for the capital's police force would be good money. He glanced down at his feet, where the tip of a toe peeked through a hole in his shoe. "If I'm going to consult," he said, "I'm going to do things my way."

This was the moment of truth. Five years ago he'd been kicked off the force for *doing things his way*. The captain was a man of rules and order. Frank's last use of heuristics had been the final straw— Captain Donovan had claimed his badge that very afternoon. But, then again, doing things his own way had always gotten Frank results.

"I figured as much," the captain responded at last. He pulled a thin folder from under his trench cloak and dropped it on Frank's desk.

"I'll be in touch," Donovan said. Then, without ceremony, he turned and left the office.

Three hours and twelve mugs of coffee later, Frank sat hunched over his desk and thumbed through the thin folder of information for the seventh time. The words jumped and swayed in the flickering candlelight, but didn't provide any new insights.

There wasn't a lot to go on. The captain had given him a list of missing documents and the duty roster for the night in question, but nothing more.

Finally, with an exaggerated sigh, Frank grabbed a piece of parchment and started making notes.

The first step in any search problem is determining what it is you hope to find—the *target*, as his old instructor in Police Algorithms 101 called it. Frank had learned that lesson early; he'd been tasked in his first week as an officer with finding the duke's prize stallion, and he'd proudly returned to the station that same afternoon with a 42-pound horned turtle. Apparently, the impressive reptile wasn't good enough. A good search algorithm means nothing if you're looking for the wrong thing.

In this case it wasn't a *what*, but rather a *who*. The captain had been right about that point. Once the thieves had the documents, it didn't matter if the police got them back. The thieves already had whatever information they needed.

So his target was simple: the person or persons who stole the documents.

The second step in any search problem is identifying the *search space*. What are you searching? During Frank's daily search for his keys, the search space was every flat surface in his office. And when

Frank wanted to find a criminal, his search space was every person in the vicinity of the capital.

Frank sat back and rubbed his eyes. It was a big search problem, finding a specific criminal in a city of criminals. But he had seen worse.

Now that he had defined the problem, he could start on an algorithm. A linear search was out; he couldn't afford to question everyone in the city. He could also rule out many of the other, fancier algorithms he had studied in the academy. For a problem like this, he would have to go back to his toolkit of basic search algorithms— the private investigator's most trusted friends.

Frank made a note on the parchment. He had the target to find, he knew the search space, and he had his algorithm. It was time to get to work.

POLICE ALGORITHMS 101: SEARCH PROBLEMS
Excerpt from Professor Drecker's Lecture

In this class we'll discuss several different algorithms (and related data structures) for solving search problems. A *search problem* is defined as any problem that requires us to find a specific value (or target) within a space of possible values (a search space).

Those of you who graduate and go on to become police officers will find yourselves facing problems that fall into this category every single day. This broad definition of a search problem encompasses a lot of different computational problems, from searching the police log for a specific entry to finding rooms within a hideout to finding all arrest records that match some criteria. This class won't be exhaustive—that would take years—but I'll give you some simple examples of basic and important algorithms as we go.

The algorithms described in this class will have three common components:

Target   The piece of data you're searching for. The target can be either a specific value or a criterion that signifies the successful completion of a search.

Search space   The set of all possibilities to test for the target. For example, the search space could be a list of values or all the nodes in a graph. A single possibility within the search space is called a *state*.

Search algorithm   The set of specific steps or instructions for conducting the search.

Some search problems will have additional requirements or complexities, which we'll touch upon as we go over different algorithms.

Exhaustive Search for an Informant

The key to efficient algorithms is information." It was Professor Drecker's mantra, barked at the cadets at the start of every Police Algorithms class, ferociously enough to sear itself permanently into Frank's memory. "A good algorithm depends on finding the structure in the data and using it. It depends on information."

Frank smiled to himself at the memory as he turned onto Three Bit Lane, a rutted dirt road lined with a combination of seedy bars and upscale coffee shops. He nodded politely to a pair of passing knights, who clanged as they jittered past in their armor, and made a mental note to grab a Triple-Bold Espresso before he left. First he needed information, something to help guide his search. He knew exactly where to start.

Glass Box Billy would be in one of the establishments by now, sitting quietly and listening to the wisps of conversation drifting through the room. People didn't mean to say things around Billy; they simply didn't notice he was there. Billy had been blessed with a single notable talent: utter inconspicuousness. Whatever he tried, there was something about Billy that meant people just didn't notice him. Maybe it was his pale skin or his small physique; maybe it was his exceptionally mundane taste in clothing. Whatever it was, Billy had long ago decided to put his one talent to use by eavesdropping, collecting information, and selling it to anyone who would buy.

Frank eyed the eight storefronts hunched together in Three Bit Lane and wondered which one Billy would have chosen. He ran through half a dozen search algorithms in his head, but it was pointless. Frank didn't have any information to go on. Billy could be in any one of the bars or coffee shops.

He'd have to use an exhaustive search—simply try all the possibilities until he found Billy. It didn't sit well with him. Years of the detective and private investigation game had taught him that there was almost always a better algorithm than exhaustive search, and he hated resorting to something so inefficient.

Grumbling, Frank started his search. He walked into the first bar on the street, The Absolute Value.

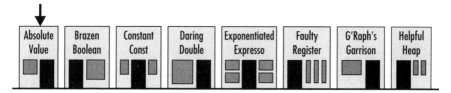

The bartender, a surly man named Abe, glared at Frank as he entered and pointedly dropped his hand below the scarred counter. The message was clear: "I am now holding a weapon. I'll let you guess what kind. But if you hassle me, I'll give you a very close look."

"I don't want any trouble, Abe," said Frank, holding up his hands. "I'm just here to see Billy."

"Well, Billy ain't here," said the barman.

Frank almost smiled in relief. "Then I'll be on my way," he said.

Abe gave a curt nod and watched Frank leave, his hand still under the counter.

Frank took a couple of deep breaths and shook his head in the cool air. Abe held a grudge longer than anyone else Frank had ever met. Then again, Frank had arrested four of his siblings.

The next establishment on the street was The Brazen Boolean, a modern coffee shop decorated in typical Boolean style—stark black and white. The inhabitants of the City of Bool were renowned for their fanatic devotion to the absolute concepts of logic, viewing everything as either True or False. They made good witnesses. As the only Boolean café in town, The Brazen Boolean was a haven for expats. After all, either you were a Boolean or you weren't.

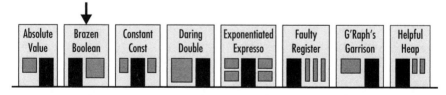

Frank popped his head in the door and asked everyone in general, "Is Billy here?" There was a brief silence as twenty pairs of eyes carefully scanned every inch of the cafe. Booleans wouldn't answer a question until they were absolutely sure.

"No," came the precise reply.

Frank continued his exhaustive search.

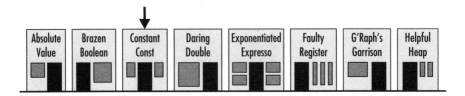

The third and fourth shops proved equally fruitless, although significantly more pleasant. The bartender of the Constant Const greeted Frank warmly and invited him in to reminisce about the good old days together, which was odd considering Frank had only met him the month before. And the crowd of the Daring Double, a notoriously loud wizards' hangout, cheered at each new arrival and sang happily over their steaming mugs.

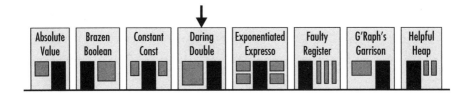

Frank found Billy in the fifth shop, the Exponentiated Expresso. It was by far the loudest and tackiest coffee shop on the street, but it managed to draw the most devoted following on account of its triply caffeinated beans. On a good day, every table would be packed with jittery people who seemed to think the key to a good conversation was volume.

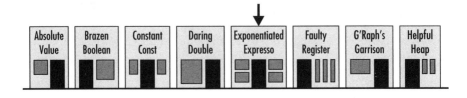

This morning, the Exponentiated Expresso hosted a comparatively subdued crowd. Only a handful of tables were occupied, and most of those by lone coffee drinkers who shook and mumbled quietly to themselves.

Billy sat at a central table, leaning awkwardly toward a nearby conversation. Nobody seemed to notice him. Frank had even missed him on his first scan of the room.

"Billy!" Frank called.

Billy jumped up guiltily. "Frank?" He grinned, happy that someone had acknowledged him, and sat back down. "Pull up a chair."

"I'm looking for some information," explained Frank as he took a seat across from Billy.

"Could be that I have some," said Billy. "I have such a hard time remembering these days," he said, glancing toward a long-empty mug that probably wasn't his.

Frank signaled the barista, who soon placed a fresh mug on the table. "Remember anything about a theft at the police station?" Frank asked Billy.

Billy's eyes widened and he flinched. "A robbery, you say?" he asked unconvincingly. His eyes darted around the room, but, as always, nobody paid him any attention.

Frank laid two gold pieces on the table, ignoring the sour feeling in his gut. He couldn't afford to spend this type of money, especially without knowing if he was paying for a lead or idle gossip. But he'd known this wasn't going to be cheap. He leaned in close. "Two nights ago," he said quietly, "the thieves took a whole pile of documents."

"Doesn't sound like the sort of thing that would be healthy to remember," said Billy. He eyed the gold pieces. "Afraid you're asking the wrong guy, Frank."

"That's gold," Frank growled.

"Sorry. I can't help you," Billy said. He surveyed the room again before adding, "Even if I did know something about a robbery, it's the sort of thing I would try to forget. Even if I did know something small, like who might have helped with logistics, it's not worth the risk of waking up to find my shoes packed with yak dung."

Frank stared, but Billy had gone silent. For someone who made a living sharing information, Billy had an odd habit of not saying things. "Yak dung?" asked Frank.

Billy nodded, but didn't offer any more.

"You couldn't be more specific, could you?" asked Frank. "Are we talking about Northern or Southern yaks?"

"Does it matter?" asked Billy. "The point is that if I knew anything about who arranged transportation, I wouldn't remember it. Especially not if those people happened to have a large farm about five miles out of town where they could easily make someone disappear. And very doubly especially if the family that owns the farm has a history of illegal activity and an unhealthy sense of humor. Nope. It definitely wouldn't be healthy to remember anything in that case."

"Too bad," Frank said with a smile. "Maybe next time then." He nodded toward the coins. "Incentive to remember things in the future."

With that, Frank stood and strode from the Exponentiated Expresso. He turned left and continued up the street. Once off Three Bit Lane, he could swing around and make for Crannock's farm— the only farm remotely matching Billy's description.

As he passed the Faulty Register, he noticed a shadow dart into a nearby alley. He cursed under his breath, but kept going. Of course he had a tail already; the captain hadn't exactly been discreet about his visit.

But by the time he left the city and was on the rough dirt lane to Crannock's farm, he found himself in a good mood. Billy hadn't given him much, but even a little information could mean the difference between an efficient search algorithm and an exhaustive one.

POLICE ALGORITHMS 101: EXHAUSTIVE SEARCH
Excerpt from Professor Drecker's Lecture

An exhaustive search algorithm searches every possibility in the entire search space for the target value. The most common exhaustive search is a *linear search*, which simply checks all the different possibilities in order.

Consider what happens when you chase a robber into the second-floor hallway of an abandoned hotel. The hall has 30 doors, all of them closed. If you've followed correct police procedures, your partner has already blocked off the opposite staircase, and the robber is trapped somewhere on that floor. How do you find him? Do you pick random doors, running back and forth until you get lucky? No! You search down the hall, kicking in one door at a time.

Or consider an algorithm that scans a list of numbers (an *array*), searching for a target value. The algorithm moves along the list from number to number, checking each value in turn so as not to miss any, and stops when it reaches the target. If we are searching an array for the number 5, then the search would progress as follows:

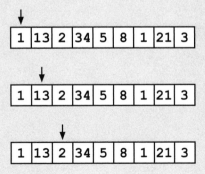

continued

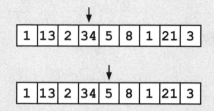

The advantage of linear search algorithms is that they are simple to implement in the field and they work even on unstructured data. You don't have to make any assumptions about which room the robber chose; you just check everything. The downside is that exhaustive algorithms are often not the most efficient algorithm if the data has structure that can be used. If you know where the robber went, you can save yourself from kicking a lot of doors by using that information.

The key to efficient algorithms is information!

Arrays and Indexes on a Criminal's Farm

Frank swore aloud when he saw the police horse tied outside Crannock's house. Since the captain had gone so far as to hire Frank in person, he hadn't expected to run into any officers. If the captain didn't trust his officers, either they were under suspicion—so he'd shuffle them to some case far across the city—or they simply weren't good enough. But, from the looks of it, someone was on the case and Frank was already behind.

He slid through the open front door and joined the officer and Mr. Crannock in the foyer. Mr. Crannock shot him a disgusted look but didn't seem surprised to see him. The officer, however, seemed caught off guard.

"Who are you?" she demanded, turning on him with parchment and quill in hand.

Frank ignored her. "Mr. Crannock," he said. "So wonderful to see you again."

"Come to harass us, too?" Crannock asked. "You're not welcome here, Frank."

"I'm not looking for a welcome," replied Frank. "I'm looking for your wife. I have a few simple questions for her."

The officer stared at him. "Frank?" she asked. "Frank Runtime? Former detective turned private eye? What are you doing here? Someone lose a pet dragon?" she scoffed.

Frank ignored her again. "Your wife, Mr. Crannock. Where can I find her?"

The old man threw up his hands. "She didn't do anything! She's gone straight, you know. For real this time." His acting wasn't half-bad for an amateur.

Frank smiled; he knew its effect was unnerving. Sure enough, Crannock cringed.

"I know that, Mr. Crannock. I'm here to tap her professional knowledge. Or I could just leave the conversation to . . ."

"Officer Notation," the young officer snapped. "And this is *my* investigation."

That was a lie. Officers always worked these investigations in pairs. More importantly, Frank recognized Notation's name from the duty roster the captain had given him. She had been at the station on the night of the crime.

"Officer Notation," Frank said. "Who said I'm here on an investigation? Maybe I'm simply searching for a lost dragon."

She scowled.

There was a commotion coming from the back of the house. Someone called for Crannock, but was cut off by a loud braying noise. "My wife is with the horses," Mr. Crannock said impatiently. "Barn #2. Now go on, get out of my house!" Crannock waved them toward the front door and scurried away through the back.

"Thank you," Frank called as he turned to leave. "Always a pleasure, Mr. Crannock."

Officer Notation followed Frank across the yard. She walked hard, stomping her anger into the ground. "Do you know where you're going?" she asked.

"Barn #2," answered Frank.

"I know that," seethed Notation. "But where is barn #2?"

Frank stopped and turned to her. "Just out of the academy, Notation?" he asked.

"What?"

"Only a rookie would ask a search question like that. Didn't you take Police Procedures and Data Structures? Or have they replaced that course with something less rigorous—Introduction to Turtle Graphics, perhaps?"

Notation seemed taken aback. "Of course I took Police Procedures and Data Structures," she said, though she sounded uncertain. "But what I meant was—"

Frank cut her off, "Then you know about arrays and indexes."

"Yes, but—" started Notation.

"Finding a barn on a farm is a simple enough search task," Frank interrupted again. "We could use an exhaustive search to check each building. *FOR EACH building on the farm: check if it is barn #2.* Back in my day, you learned that search on the first day of Police Algorithms.

"But we can do better here. The Crannocks have six barns in a nice line—just like a giant array. Mr. Crannock was kind enough to supply us with the barn number, the index into that array. All we have to do is walk to the corresponding barn."

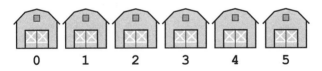

"That's not what I meant!" shouted Notation, waving her arms. "I know how to use the index of an array. I know that we only have to walk up to the barn with a giant #2 outside. I graduated first in my class in both Data Structures *and* Police Algorithms, so don't lecture me on the correct use of arrays."

"Well, you asked," Frank replied.

"What I was asking is: Do you know where this wonderful array of barns is located?"

"Of course you were," said Frank. He began walking again. "You still sound like a rookie, though, quoting class rank."

"Where are the barns?" shouted the officer, stamping to catch up.

Frank shot her a smile over his shoulder. "Over this hill."

As Frank had learned years ago, the Crannock family embraced the concept of arrays with an almost fanatical devotion. They organized everything into linear structures with clearly labeled indexes for each element. As he passed barn #0, Frank noted 15 pig troughs, each capable of storing one serving of food. A farm hand was iterating down the line and ladling out the next meal into each array location.

Frank and Officer Notation moved on to barn #2, labeled with a sign outside its door. Mrs. Crannock's icy greeting was almost pleasant, compared to previous encounters; she hadn't even thrown anything . . . yet.

"What do you want?" Mrs. Crannock demanded.

"Mrs. Crannock," Notation cut in before Frank could steal her witness. "I was hoping I could ask you a few questions."

Frank let Officer Notation ask the questions. Billy's clue hadn't yielded anything more than a lead to the farm, but Notation appeared to be working from a better collection of clues.

Mrs. Crannock sneered and spat on the ground. "I didn't do anything," she said. "I've gone straight, you know."

"I'm not here to arrest you," said Notation. "I need to ask you about a certain donkey cart—the ArrayCart?"

A flicker of doubt went through Frank. Could Officer Notation be here for a different case? He doubted it. His gut told him that she was after the lost documents, and he had learned to trust his gut.

"The ArrayCart," said Mrs. Crannock suspiciously, though with the barest note of pride. "My own invention. Based it off of an array. It's got individual storage pens for our animals. Each pen stores exactly one animal. Since they all have separate doors, you can walk up to any pen and take an animal out or put one in. Easy access to any storage location. Saves hours of wrangling."

"It's quite ingenious," Officer Notation conceded. "You've found a way to apply the concept of arrays and indexes to livestock transportation."

"And that's just the beginning," added Mrs. Crannock. "I'm working with a certain *wizard* on a completely new type of ArrayCart— one with magical pointers! I bet they'd be perfect for the police force. Tell your captain that I can give him a good price."

Frank had to hand it to Notation. The surest way to get a Crannock talking was to bring up arrays.

"You have a few ArrayCarts that you rent out now. Is that correct?" probed Officer Notation.

Mrs. Crannock's eyes became instantly cold. "It's a legitimate business. We pay our taxes."

Frank held back a derisive snort.

"Did you happen to rent an ArrayCart to anyone two nights ago?" pressed Officer Notation. "A smaller model with six pens."

"I might've," said Mrs. Crannock. Her cold demeanor was creeping toward hostile.

"Do you have a record of who rented it?" asked the officer.

"No," said Mrs. Crannock. "We shred the records once the carts are returned. I don't happen to recall who rented that one."

It seemed like Billy's hint had paid off. If you were a criminal in need of transportation, there were few places that would rent you a cart, and fewer still that would forget your name afterward. Mrs. Crannock may have claimed to have gone straight, but apparently she still, at the very least, provided a valuable service to her former associates.

"Are you sure you don't remember anything about your customer?" prompted Officer Notation, but Frank knew it was pointless. He had once questioned her for three hours about a stolen yak. She hadn't given him a single peep, despite being the one who had been robbed. Mrs. Crannock wouldn't talk.

While Officer Notation tried a few variations of the same question, Frank quietly slipped out of the barn and found the cart lot. As he expected, the lot was organized as an array with 10 labeled parking spots. Only spots #2, #4, and #8 were occupied. The carts in positions #2 and #4 had 10 pens apiece, so were too large to fit Notation's description. But slot #8 held a six-pen ArrayCart, its wheels still coated with fresh mud.

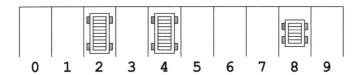

After a quick glance around, Frank heaved himself into the back of the six-pen ArrayCart. A scattering of straw covered the floor, but the cart was otherwise empty. Frank opened each pen in turn, scanning the empty storage spaces for any clues. Then, getting down on his hands and knees, he sifted through the straw until he found a few scraps of parchment.

He collected six tiny pieces in all, probably corners that had caught on nails as the scrolls were unloaded. Only two of the pieces contained writing, and those appeared to be from ledgers. It wasn't exactly a solid lead, but it tied the cart to the crime.

Frank moved his search to the front of the cart, carefully inspecting everything around the driver's seat. The seat itself gave him his first real clue. There he found a few black and orange threads caught by the seat's splintered wood. From the vividness of the colors alone, Frank could tell the cloak must have been new. Satisfied, he pocketed the threads and stepped down from the cart.

Only when a gust of fresh air hit him did he notice he'd been holding his breath. Around the cart was a stench of rotting fish. He sniffed lightly, following the smell, and arrived at the mud-caked wheels. He took a great, deep sniff and immediately regretted it. The smell of rotting eel emanating from the mud was as unmistakable as it was unpleasant.

Frank half-smiled, half-gagged as he staggered back from the cart. He might not know who had rented it, but now he knew where it had been.

POLICE ALGORITHMS 101: ARRAYS
Excerpt from Professor Drecker's Lecture

Arrays are simple data structures that allow you to store multiple values. An array is like a row of bins. Each bin can store a single piece of information, such as a number or a character.

Value:	20	15	19	1	10	1	5	33	9
Index:	0	1	2	3	4	5	6	7	8

The structure of an array means you can access any value (or element) within the array, whether to write to it or read from it, by specifying its location, or *index*, within the array. Many programming languages use 0-indexed arrays, which means the first value of the array resides at index 0, the second at index 1, and so forth. Commonly, you reference the value at index i of array A as $A[i]$; for example, the third element of array A would be $A[2]$ and equal to 19.

You likely recognize this structure from your introductory tour of the holding cells in the capital's police station yesterday. The king personally suggested the use of indexed, single-person cells to streamline the retrieval of prisoners. Each station is equipped with an array of four to eight holding cells, depending on the size of the local criminal population.

Strings and Hidden Messages

Frank shook off Officer Notation and left through the back gate of the farm, where a large sign faced the road. For years the Crannocks had used this sign to broadcast coded messages about various illegal activities. These days it was something of a tourist attraction for visiting criminals—a place thugs took their younger protégés and gathered to reminisce about stories that invariably began "Back in my day . . ."

The sign itself was an AnyText model. It held 3 arrays of letters, each array with 12 slots. Each letter, space, or punctuation mark took up a single slot in an array, meaning the board could hold a total of 36 individual characters—enough to advertise a whole range of illegal activities. Every Monday morning, one of the Crannocks would drag a basket of letters to the sign and individually place the appropriate character in each slot of the array.

During his first week on the force, Frank's partner had brought him out here to "check the board." The message at the time—*Apple picker wanted. Got slugs?*—sounded innocuous enough to Frank. The Crannocks were looking for an apple picker to help with the harvest and were offering to get rid of people's slugs. When he said this to his partner, a 20-year veteran, she laughed.

```
| A | P | P | L | E |   | P | I | C | K | E | R |   |
| W | A | N | T | E | D | . |   |   |   |   |   |   |
| G | O | T |   | S | L | U | G | S | ? |   |   |   |
```

"That's what they want you to think," Detective Rossile explained. "You have to look beyond the obvious meaning and see what the criminal mind would see. In this case, *Apple picker wanted* indicates that they are trying to hire a petty thief. Someone who would steal apples from a cart or such."

"And the slugs?" Frank asked.

"Illegal slug racing," she replied. "They hold races here every few months. You'll get to know that one."

Thus, Frank had learned to check the Crannocks' board weekly to get a pulse on the criminal world. After the first few months, he had learned to decipher most of the codes. *Farmhands* meant henchmen, with additional modifiers if strength, brutality, or just plain numbers were needed. A *print artist* referred to a forger, while a *vocal artist* was a con man, and so forth. The phrase *a flock of chickens* had stumped Frank for a few days before Rossile translated it as "a large number of warm bodies to run around noisily and cause a distraction; no intelligence required."

By the end of his first year, Frank had become an expert at reading the board. The only time in the past few years that Frank had a hard time deciphering a criminal tip from the board was during the wizard Exponentious's attack on the kingdom. Exponentious had unleashed the Spell of Incorrect Indexes on all the kingdom's ArrayDesignBoards. As its name implied, the spell changed the indexes, so the locations Mrs. Crannock thought she was setting the letters to were wrong. For a week, the Crannocks' board held gibberish.

D	E	F		V	E	I	N	S			E	
D	I	Z					W	A	R			
D	E	N	T						A	W		

Since the spell only mixed up letters within an array and the AnyText model was implemented as three separate arrays, Frank had to unscramble each line individually. He puzzled out the message: *Defensive wizard wanted.*

Today, though, the message was clear. In fact, it was the least subtle message he had ever seen on the Crannocks' board. It read *ArrayCarts for rent. No questions.*

POLICE ALGORITHMS 101: STRINGS
Excerpts from Professor Drecker's Lecture

Arrays don't just store lists of numbers; they can also be used to store strings of text characters. Many programming languages implement strings using arrays. Each block in the array holds a single character, which can be a letter, number, symbol, or space. As with arrays of other data, characters in these strings can be accessed directly through their index in the array.

Value:	H	E	L	L	O	!
Index:	0	1	2	3	4	5

During your career in the police force, you will come to know this representation of text *very* well. All standard police forms require officers to record their names within a 32-block array at the top of *each* page. In a typical month, you will fill in over 400 such arrays.

Binary Search for a Smuggler's Ship

The port of Usb was little more than a fishing village. A dozen weathered buildings clustered around the end of a single long pier. A few pockets of meager activity surrounded the most recent arrivals, but otherwise the town was reassuringly quiet.

Frank headed straight for the Crab's Pinch, a fisherman's bar renowned for its clam chowder and Wednesday night sea shanty contests. With any luck, one of his contacts would turn up before the day was out. After all, the Crab's Pinch was the only place to go in Usb. So Frank planted himself at a table in the back corner, ordered the chowder, and waited.

It wasn't long before a freelance smuggler named Mavis entered the dank little bar. Careful by nature, Mavis had never technically been convicted of a crime, though it was well-known that she'd once set her own ship on fire to destroy evidence. Frank got along with her well enough, at least once he'd left the force, and they even exchanged the occasional scrap of information.

Frank, having nursed his chowder for a solid hour, finally pushed away his bowl and motioned to Mavis. She hesitated a moment by the door before jostling her way through the bar.

"Mavis," said Frank as she joined him in the corner, "how are you?"

"I was doing a lot better 10 minutes ago," she spat.

Before Frank could ask, Officer Notation strode through the door and held up her hands. "Ladies and gentlemen," she called. "If I could have your attention for a moment. I'm looking for a cart that came through here two nights ago."

Frank cursed under his breath. So much for his lead.

"I come in from the dawn run, hoping for a bowl of hot chowder and a few minutes of peace," Mavis complained. "Instead I get this copper clammering about donkey carts."

Frank laughed dryly. "And until she goes away, you can't unload your cargo. Right?"

Mavis scowled at him but didn't object. Usb had never found success in either the fishing or shipping industries. The port did, however, appeal to those criminals concerned with moving merchandise without dealing with nosy government officials. Frank would wager a month's rent that there wasn't a single ship at dock that wasn't smuggling something.

"Do you know anything about the cart?" Frank dropped his voice to just above a whisper.

Mavis shrugged. "There's always carts on the docks. This is a port, Frank. People move things."

"This is a special cart," Frank pressed. "A bunch of individual animal pens, like a giant array on wheels."

"Sounds fancy," said Mavis. "But I haven't heard of any ships moving animals. I might have heard a rumor about a crate or two of miniature turtles, but nothing large enough to need a pen. You sure it came through here?"

Frank nodded. The smell had been like a fish-scented air freshener in an outhouse, and few places smelled as bad as Usb.

"Anybody casting off at that time?" he asked. If the thieves had transported the stolen documents this far, they wouldn't have waited around.

"Only the *Retry Loop*," said Mavis. "And I'm only telling you that because it's public knowledge. I don't know what it was carrying, and I don't care."

"Do you know when it returns?" asked Frank.

"Got back into port 19 hours ago," replied Mavis. "Don't know what it was carrying then either."

Frank smiled widely. "Sounds like it's time for me to take a stroll around town," he said.

Mavis smiled halfheartedly at him and turned to flag down a waiter.

Frank made it less than 20 meters down the pier before Officer Notation marched up beside him.

"Mr. Runtime, this is my investigation," she began. "If you have information—"

Frank stopped, causing her to pull up short. "What exactly are you investigating, Officer?" he asked.

It was better than Frank had hoped. Notation opened and closed her mouth a few times as a red flush spread up her neck.

"The captain doesn't know you're here, does he?" Frank asked. "This isn't exactly an *official* investigation."

"I don't know what you're—" started Officer Notation, but Frank cut her off.

"Cut the act," he said. "The fact you're out here alone is all the proof I need. You're running this investigation on your own time. The question is, why?"

The flush had now finished its ascent of Officer Notation's face. Her ears burned a particularly vivid shade of red.

"That's none of your concern," she said.

"It is when the captain comes to me because he can't trust his own officers," Frank replied calmly.

"The *captain* hired a washed-up gumshoe like *you*?"

"Yes. Because he can trust *me*."

Officer Notation's face grew hard and her eyes burned. For a second, Frank thought she might end this conversation with her billy club. But almost as quickly as her anger had flared, it deflated.

"I need to recover those documents," she said mournfully. "It was my fault—I was on guard duty that night."

"I see," said Frank thoughtfully.

"I need to recover those documents," repeated Officer Notation, sounding agitated. "I've only been on the force for a few months and—"

Frank cut her off and gave her what he hoped was a reassuring smile. This was what he had expected. Rookies rarely dealt well with their first mistakes, and Notation seemed more tightly wound than most. "We're looking for the *Retry Loop*," he said. "The Crannocks' cart unloaded something there the night of the robbery. The ship docked 19 hours ago."

He didn't trust her, of course, but he wanted to keep her close, keep an eye on her. The fact that she had found the Crannocks meant she knew more than she had put in her report. Something was missing from her story, and he needed to find out what else she knew.

"We better get started," said Notation, looking worriedly down the pier. "There are a lot of ships to check. Should we start at the front?" As most of the vessels in port belonged to smugglers, none of them displayed identification. They would have to ask each ship's name in turn.

"We can do better than that," Frank explained. "The harbormaster is fanatical about organization. He insists that the docked ships be sorted in order of their arrival time. The newest arrival gets a prime spot near town, where the crew can easily load and unload, but when a new ship arrives, the rest of them are forced to shift down to give it space in front."

"That's absurd," protested Notation. "What a tremendous amount of wasted effort. Why would he do that?"

Frank chuckled. "He claims it's for efficiency, but anyone who's spent a week in Usb knows the truth. The harbormaster can't stand the smell of rotting fish. Ships that remain in harbor without selling their loads become, well . . . fragrant. The harbormaster's organizational scheme moves the ones that have been here longer away from his shack."

Officer Notation stared at him. "Are you serious?" she asked finally.

Frank chuckled again. "Yes. You'll start picking up these useful bits of information, too, once you've walked the beat awhile. The point is that we know the ships are in sorted order and we know the *Retry Loop* has been here for 19 hours, so we can just do a *binary search*.

"Our target value is 19, and our algorithm is binary search. Right now the search space is that whole line of ships, so we already have an upper and lower bound. If we use inclusive bounds, our lower bound is the first ship and our upper bound is the last ship. If the *Retry Loop* is here, it obviously can't be in front of the first ship or after the last ship.

"So we start with the middle ship and ask how long it's been in port. If it's been there less than 19 hours, then it must come before the *Retry Loop*. That will split our search space in two. And—"

"If it's been there more than 19 hours, then it must come after the *Retry Loop*," interrupted Notation. "I know about binary search. My Police Algorithms final was just two and a half months ago."

With that, the two of them set off in search of the *Retry Loop*. The middle ship, a yellow schooner that smelled oddly of bananas, had been in port for 17 hours.

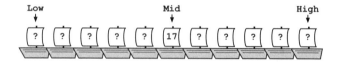

That meant they could rule out the half of the ships at the front, including the middle ship. Frank adjusted the lower bound to the first ship that *could* be the *Retry Loop,* one ship past the yellow schooner.

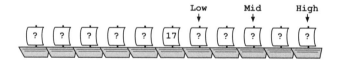

With the reduced search space, they chose a new middle point. It took a while to convince the captain of the next ship that they weren't undercover customs officials. After 10 minutes, Notation shoved her badge under the captain's nose, and his tone changed immediately to an irate whine as he informed them that his ship, the *Corrupt Packet,* had been stuck in port for 22 agonizing hours. He demanded they speak to the harbormaster on his behalf.

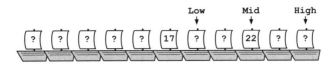

Since their target was 19 hours, they knew the *Retry Loop* would have to come before the *Corrupt Packet*. They changed the bounds again so that the ship to the left of the *Corrupt Packet* was now the upper bound.

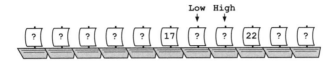

This left only two ships in the search range; they were rapidly nearing the end of the search. If neither of these ships was the *Retry Loop*, they would know for certain that it had left port, as once there were no more elements in the search space, they could rule out the entire search space.

Since there were only two ships left, they could choose either as their new middle point. Going with his gut, Frank picked the earlier ship, which happened to also be their lower bound. A quick chat with a crewmember loitering on the pier confirmed that the ship was indeed the *Retry Loop* and it had been in port for 19 hours.

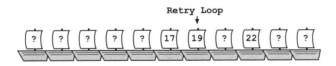

"Now what?" asked Officer Notation as they stood watching the ship.

"We use your shiny badge again," Frank replied.

POLICE ALGORITHMS 101: BINARY SEARCH
Excerpts from Professor Drecker's Lecture

A binary search algorithm is used to efficiently find a target value v in a sorted array A. Unlike in a linear scan, a binary search uses information about the structure of the data to make the search more efficient. The key to efficient algorithms is information. In this case, we use the fact that the array is sorted in increasing order:

$A[i] \leq A[j]$ for any pair of indexes i and j such that $i < j$

This might not seem like a lot of information, but it's enough to make the search more efficient.

The binary search algorithm works by repeatedly dividing the search space in half and limiting the search to only one of those halves. The algorithm limits the active search space by tracking two bounds. The upper bound (*IndexHigh*) marks the highest index of the array that's part of the active search space. The lower bound (*IndexLow*) marks the lowest index. Throughout the algorithm, if the target value is in the array, we guarantee the following:

$A[IndexLow] \leq v \leq A[IndexHigh]$

At each step in the search, we check the value halfway between the lower and upper bounds:

$$IndexMid = \frac{IndexHigh + IndexLow}{2}$$

We can then compare the value at this middle location, $A[IndexMid]$, with the target value, v. If the middle point is less than the target value, $A[IndexMid] < v$, we know that the target value must lie after the middle index. This allows us to chop the search space in half again by making $IndexLow = IndexMid + 1$.

If the middle point is greater than the target value, $A[IndexMid] > v$, we know the target value must lie before the middle index, which allows us to chop the search space in half by making $IndexHigh = IndexMid - 1$.

Of course, if we find $A[IndexMid]$ equals v, we can immediately conclude the search. We found the target.

Let's consider searching the following (sorted) array for the value 15. The boxes with dotted outlines correspond to the values the algorithm has checked, and the shaded elements are ones that have been eliminated from the search.

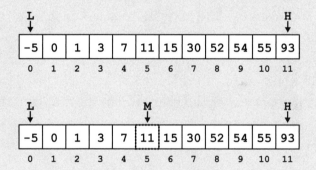

The first midpoint check finds a value of 11, which is less than our target value of 15. Since we know the array is sorted in increasing order, we can rule out the midpoint and anything before it. We move our lower bound index appropriately ($IndexLow = IndexMid + 1$).

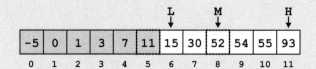

continued

Similarly, after the second comparison, we find a midpoint value of 52, which is greater than the target value. We can rule out the midpoint and everything after it. We move our upper bound index (*IndexHigh* = *IndexMid* − 1).

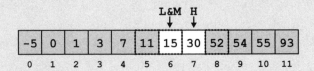

Note that even though the lower bound's index pointed to the target value ($v = 15$) for several iterations, we continued the search until the midpoint pointed to the target value. This is because our search checks only the value at the midpoint. We don't check the values at the lower or upper indexes until the midpoint reaches them.

What happens if the target value is not in the array? As the search progresses, the bounds will move closer until there are no unexplored values between them. Since we are always moving one of the bounds *past* the midpoint index, we can stop the search when *IndexHigh* < *IndexLow*. At that point we can guarantee the target value is not in the array.

Binary Search for Clues

F ood inspectors," Frank called out as he and Officer Notation stepped up the narrow gangplank and onto the ship. At Frank's instigation, Notation waved her badge in a blur, too fast for anyone to read.

"Food inspectors?" asked a crew member. "We aren't transporting any food."

Frank looked the man over. He wasn't an officer or hired security, probably just a sailor who had taken charge while the officers were away. It wasn't uncommon. Smugglers rarely employed guards to watch their ships. It drew too much attention.

Frank turned on the sailor, growling out his words. "We'll see about that. I'm told there's a load of rotting eels on this dock, and I intend to find them."

"Eels?" The sailor was clearly out of his depth.

"*Rotting* eels," Frank shot back. "We're going down to check the stores." Then, without waiting for a response, he strode to the hatch leading below deck.

Notation hurried after him.

"We don't have much time before they get the captain. We need to find the logbook," Frank said as he climbed down the ladder. The logbook would contain a manifest of items shipped and a list of ports visited. The manifest would be fake, of course. Smuggling ships never documented their true cargo. But with any luck, he could read between the lies and find a clue.

Officer Notation found the logbook at the back of the hold and pulled it out. Frank checked the cover and swore:

> Manifest and Log of the *Retry Loop*
> Captain: A. James
> Home Port: Usb
> Owner: Vinettees Shipping Group LLC

After months of successfully avoiding the Vinettees, Frank had walked right onto one of their ships. He found himself reflexively scanning the hold for hidden henchmen, stashes of weaponized farm equipment, or evidence of a slug racetrack. Frank discarded the last possibility—everyone knew slugs wouldn't race on a ship; it had something to do with being surrounded by large quantities of saltwater.

He shook his head and focused on the problem at hand. Frank had to find a clue before the Vinettees knew he was on the ship, or he might not get back off again. He turned to the end of the book and started flipping toward the front, one page at a time.

"What are you doing?" asked Notation.

"Looking for the last entry," said Frank.

"One page at a time?" asked Notation. "There's got to be a thousand pages. Why don't you use binary search again? We just used it two minutes ago."

Frank paused. He wasn't looking for a specific page number, but he could still use a binary search to find the last entry. He would just refine the search bounds depending on whether the current page had text or not.

"Okay. Binary search," he agreed.

He opened to the last page again and confirmed the book had exactly 1,000 pages, giving him a lower bound of page 1 and an upper bound of page 1,000. He added the numbers, divided by 2, and computed a midpoint of 500. He flipped to that page.

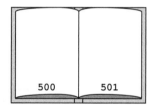

Pages 500 and 501 were both blank, so Frank knew the last written page was on or before 499—his new upper bound. After another midpoint computation, he flipped to page 250. Again it was blank.

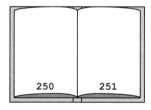

"Looks like a new book," added Notation. "Good thing you didn't keep going from the back."

Frank didn't bother replying. With a lower bound of 1 and an upper bound of 249, he computed a midpoint of 125. This time he found writing, so he adjusted his lower bound accordingly to 125.

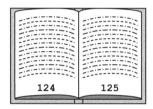

"187," supplied Notation before Frank could finish the midpoint computation in his head. He turned to 187, again finding writing and adjusting his lower bound.

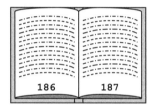

"218," said Notation. The pages were blank, so Frank adjusted his lower and upper bounds to 187 and 217, respectively.

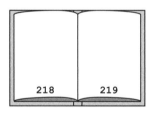

"202," said Notation before Frank had even finished adding the upper and lower bounds.

"How are you doing that so fast?" asked Frank.

"Practice," she replied. "We used to have binary search competitions at the academy whenever we needed a break from studying. I was undefeated."

Frank shook his head. "Sounds like a wild time," he muttered.

Pages 202 and 203 were filled. "210," supplied Notation.

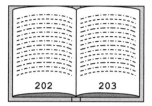

At page 210, they finally found the last entry, detailing the *Retry Loop*'s last voyage. "What now?" asked Notation.

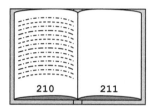

"We search for an interesting package or port. On the last voyage, they made about 70 entries. We'll have to scan through them."

"Exhaustive search?" asked Notation. "Can't we use something more efficient? Aren't the entries sorted by pickup and delivery time?"

"The sorting doesn't help us here," answered Frank. "We don't know the time. Sorted data only helps when it's sorted by a useful dimension. They didn't bother to sort by suspiciousness. Go figure."

"Oh. It's the Weather Records problem," said Notation.

"What problem?" asked Frank.

"It's an illustration of how sorting data by the wrong value doesn't help a search," explained Notation. "Professor Drecker gave the example of finding the coldest day in the last 10 years. If the logs are sorted by day, you can use binary search to efficiently find any specific day. But that doesn't help us to find the coldest day, so we'd still have to scan through all the data. I hadn't expected to see such a clear example outside of class, though."

"Welcome to the real world," said Frank. "Out here, you have to check when the structure in the data is helpful to you and when it isn't. Don't worry, it's a common rookie mistake."

He could see Notation bristle at his words and tried not to enjoy her reaction too much. Every rookie came out of the academy thinking they knew it all, and every one had a lot to learn. Notation was getting off easy with a lecture. His own education with binary search had involved hours of scooping through barrels of pig waste while he questioned his career choice.

After about three minutes, they found their only clue. The *Retry Loop* had recently made two suspicious stops, at the Port of Mudwall and Frayed Cable Island. Even for smugglers, these were strange destinations. The Port of Mudwall boasted little trade beyond its outlying mud farms. And Frayed Cable Island was even more desolate; the small, rocky island possessed only a single building—the now abandoned Iron Ring Prison.

"There," said Frank, pointing. "That's where they took your documents. Either the Port of Mudwall or Frayed Cable Island. They probably dropped the documents off at one and picked up the payment at the other."

"How do you know?" asked Notation. She looked skeptical. "Shouldn't we consider all the ports as—"

Frank cut her off. "No time to check them all." He didn't elaborate. He was using his own brand of algorithm now, the heuristic searches that had gotten him in trouble with the captain in the past. But he had a gut feeling, and Frank had learned to trust his gut.

"Are you sure that—" Notation began, but was cut off by noises above them.

Frank couldn't make out the words, but he could recognize the tone clearly. Trouble was on its way.

POLICE ALGORITHMS 101: BINARY SEARCH II
Excerpts from Professor Drecker's Lecture

The key to efficient algorithms is information. In the case of binary search, we require that the data be sorted and that we have information on how that data is sorted. In order to rule out (or prune) large regions of the search space, the algorithm must be able to guarantee that the target value can't be in that region. We can only do that if we know how the values behave as we move along the array. In computational problems, we say the array is sorted if all its values are arranged in increasing (or decreasing) order.

However, just because the data is sorted by *one* dimension doesn't mean that you will be able to binary search along another dimension. Say you're searching an accounting ledger for clues. Ledgers are sorted by transaction number, which indicates when the transaction was *recorded*. This means that the transaction number for each entry will be less than the transaction number for the following entry. If the current entry has a transaction number of 105, we know that all entries before it will have transaction numbers less than 105 and all entries after it will have transaction numbers greater than 105.

101	August 16	Zed's Coffee	8.00
102	August 15	Bob's Pizza	20.00
103	August 15	Wands and More	150.00
104	August 15	Spell Shoppe	100.00
105	August 16	Zed's Coffee	8.00
106	August 16	Spell Shoppe	50.00
107	August 17	Zed's Coffee	8.00
108	August 17	Hospital	250.00

continued

However, this also means that the entries in other fields, such as the actual date of the transaction, the mechant's name, or the transaction amount, are *not* in sorted order. What if you're interested in finding transactions above a certain suspicious amount or with a known weapons merchant? Does the sorting help you here? No, you would still find yourself using an exhaustive linear search. Knowing that transaction 105 was at Zed's Coffee doesn't tell you anything about the merchants or amounts in transactions before or after that one.

Similarly, if you sorted the ledger in increasing order of transaction amount, this would allow you to quickly find all transactions costing $250, but it would not help you search for a given transaction date, ID, or merchant.

Adapting Algorithms for a Daring Escape

Heavy footsteps pounded the wooden deck above. Frank glanced around, assessing their limited options. The only hatch led up to the deck and the new arrivals. The hold itself was nearly empty, the crew having unloaded the cargo upon arriving in Usb. Trying to hide here would amount to standing in a corner and whispering "You can't see me."

As Frank listed and discarded every possible option, including the rarely effective ploy of lying down and playing dead, he saw Notation pull out her badge and stand at attention.

"What are you thinking?" he hissed.

"I am an officer of the law on an official investigation," explained Notation.

Frank shook his head in disbelief. "The 'Stop in the name of the law' routine isn't about to work here. Or most places, for that matter. We're on a smuggler's ship, investigating the theft of police property. No one on the force even knows you're here, do they? And I'd be willing to bet whoever is coming through that door knows that."

Notation opened her mouth to argue, but paused and closed it again. She slid her badge back into her jacket as a stream of large and surprisingly well-dressed thugs poured through the door. They spread out in the hold and formed a loose circle around Frank and Notation.

"Ladies and gentlemen," said Frank. "We have concluded our inspection and it appears that you are not carrying any rotting eels. Thank you for your patience as we strive to ensure the safety of this kingdom's food supply. We'll be on our way now."

By way of reply, two of the larger thugs grabbed Frank's arms. Together they lifted him off the ground and proceeded to carry him back up onto the deck. Years of experience had prepared Frank for this reaction and he had developed a technique for positioning himself so as to minimize discomfort, but he could still almost feel the bruises forming under their powerful grip.

"Hey!" Notation's shout indicated that she was being similarly escorted outside.

Frank blinked as they emerged into the sunlight. The men carried him to the middle of the deck and dumped him on the wooden floor. Notation thudded next to him, and the thugs again formed a loose circle around them.

Frank slowly pushed himself into a sitting position and eyed their captors. They swayed with the ship but otherwise didn't move. They appeared to be waiting, which meant that whoever was in charge hadn't arrived yet. Frank seized the opportunity and turned to the nearest thug.

"What's the plan then?" asked Frank. "Lock us away? Drop us over the side? Hand us over to your boss's employer?"

The man shrugged. "Don't look at me, I've only been working here for fifteen days."

"A newbie, huh?" said Frank.

The Vinettees were fanatical about limiting information. They only shared their plans with the most senior person on the crew. New hires were required to prove their loyalty as they worked their way up the ranks. To get any useful information, Frank would need to find the most senior person aboard.

A plan started to form in Frank's mind. The Vinettees' crews always arranged themselves in order of seniority. It had something to do with mentorship—the most junior crew member served as a new hire's mentor and so forth up the ranks. In group situations, they all tended to stand next to their mentors.

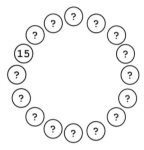

The circle of thugs was nothing more than a sorted array that had been bent into a loop. Binary search would almost work here, but it would have to be adapted to fit the organization of the data: a circle, rather than a straight line of values. Unfortunately, this meant that Frank didn't know where the array started or ended. Quickly he developed a new algorithm to efficiently search for the most senior crew member. In this case, efficiency meant both minimizing the number of thugs with whom he would have to converse and maximizing his chances of getting answers before they caught on.

He turned to the woman on the thug's right. "How about you? Are you the veteran here then?"

"Nineteen days," she said.

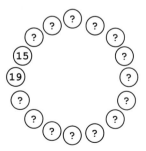

Now Frank expected that he had an ordering—that seniority increased as he went counterclockwise around the circle. But he couldn't be sure yet. As absurd as the possibility was, Fifteen-Days and Nineteen-Days could be the most junior and senior thugs, respectively. He had been careless with choosing how to start searches before; it never ended well. He need another data point. So he chose the middle of the remaining range of thugs.

"How about you?" he asked a woman across from Fifteen-Days.

"Thirty-seven days," replied the thug. "What's it to you?"

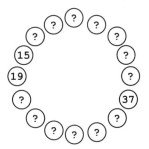

With this piece of information, his hunch of a counterclockwise ordering was confirmed. Therefore, he discarded everyone between Fifteen-Days and the person before Thirty-Seven-Days from consideration—the most senior thug, if it wasn't Thirty-Seven-Days, would have to be counterclockwise from her, but before Fifteen-Days.

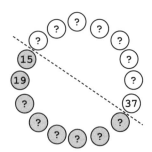

Frank stifled a rising swell of annoyance. He had never faced such a junior crew before. He actually felt a little insulted. "This is getting embarrassing," Frank said to their captors. "We were caught by a bunch of newbies. What are you all, the backup team?"

"What are you doing?" whispered Notation.

"A modified binary search," Frank growled back.

Notation sighed. "I figured that out. It looks like you're searching for the most senior one. You're not exactly being subtle. But why? And how do you know they're standing in order?"

Frank ignored her. He took a deep breath and refocused on the task at hand. He didn't know how much time he had before The Boss showed up. He chose the middle of the remaining range. "And you?"

"This is my third day," replied the man, hesitantly.

"Come on!" shouted Frank. "Really?"

"Three days? You're not in training or anything?" Notation asked, sounding genuinely curious.

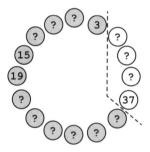

Frank refined his range again, accounting for the fact that the most senior person couldn't be Three-Days, Fifteen-Days, or anyone in between.

Frank divided the remaining range in half again. "You must be a relative veteran then, right?" Frank asked.

"Uh . . . this is my first day, sir," stammered the thug. He began sweating profusely as everyone's attention turned to him.

Frank cursed under his breath.

"Don't call him sir," shouted Nineteen-Days. "He's our prisoner."

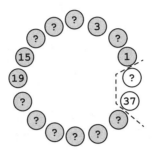

Frank had now limited the search to a very small window. "And I suppose this is your first day too?" he asked the last thug under consideration. He didn't bother hiding his disdain.

The woman laughed. "I've been with the Vinettees for over a month," she said. "Forty-two days of keeping nosy cops out of the way."

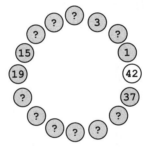

Bingo. "Really?" said Frank. "What are you doing here then?"

The thug frowned. "What do you mean?"

"The Vinettees usually reserve their senior henchmen for more important tasks. Babysitting a shipment of smuggled cabbages seems like a waste of your time," he said, struggling to remember whether there had been anything about cabbages in the log. It was a reasonable bluff anyway. All smugglers dealt in cabbages at some point. The recent increase in cabbage taxes had practically doubled the black market trade in Usb.

"Cabbages?" the woman scoffed. "I did the cabbage route on my first day. We have more important work now."

"Really?" said Frank. "Move all the way up to carrots?"

The thug turned a bright shade of red. Even though they often accounted for over 80 percent of a smuggler's profit, somehow vegetable smuggling remained the embarrassing side of the business.

"No," she said. "A hundred times better than carrots. A private contract."

"Really?" said Frank. "I hear that fencing carrots is good business. Pays well, they say."

"Oh, don't worry about that," said the thug with an air of smugness. "The League pays us well for our service. We were told—"

"Mr. Runtime." A familiar voice cut through the air. "Stop trying to weasel information out of my employees. You will find that the information is no more useful than it is challenging to procure. They, of course, know nothing of value."

Frank looked up to see Rebecca Vinettee join the circle. His stomach clenched.

"And you are?" prompted Vinettee, looking at Officer Notation.

"This is Susan Pointer from the Bureau of Food Safety, Pickled Eel Division," said Frank. "We're looking into a bad shipment of Usb Greytails."

Rebecca Vinettee made a soft tsking sound. "No, Mr. Runtime. I don't think so." She paused, studying Notation carefully. "If I am not mistaken, this is Officer Elizabeth Notation. First year on the police force."

"I'm on an official—" started Notation.

"No," interrupted Rebecca Vinettee. "You are not on an official investigation, Officer Notation. I know all the officers currently assigned to official investigations, from grand theft aquatic all the way down to slug racing. My sources keep me well informed about such things, and you are not on any of their lists. But you *are* trespassing on my ship. So the question is what to do with you?"

"I thought the question was 'why?'" said Frank.

"Mr. Runtime," said Rebecca Vinettee with exaggerated patience. "Please do not underestimate me. I know the why. I knew the why before you did. I also know the who, when, what, and even the how.

"But the question remains, how should I deal with two nosy officers—oh, my apologies. You are an officer no longer, are you, Frank? I should ask: How should I deal with a nosy officer and a nosy disgraced former officer?"

Frank clenched his fists. His thoughts flashed back to his last month on the force and Rebecca's mocking laugh as she was released from the cells. He hadn't been able to build a case, at least not while following the book, and the captain had been forced to let her go.

"How about you bore us to death with a monologue?" asked Frank. "Why don't you tell us about the League?"

Rebecca laughed. "Don't worry, Mr. Runtime, I have no intention of keeping you around long enough to bore. I had, of course, already decided how to deal with you, if you ever chanced to get in my way again. The question was merely a kindness to give you the illusion of control over your own demise."

"Demise?" Notation squeaked.

Rebecca Vinettee nodded at the circle of henchmen, and they advanced, drawing an assortment of fancy weaponry from their expensive suits like magicians performing elaborate conjuring acts. One tall man produced a three-foot-long spiked club from under his tie; another thug slide a broadsword out of her sleeve.

Then, to absolutely everyone's surprise, a barrel landed on the deck with a loud *thwack* and burst open, spraying pickled eels across the planks.

POLICE ALGORITHMS 101:
ADAPTING YOUR BINARY SEARCH
Excerpt from Professor Drecker's Lecture

Not every computational problem you face during your career is going to have a nice, prepackaged solution. Sure, scholars have spent years studying a vast range of problems and writing up solutions. But in the field you'll find new problems with new wrinkles. If you leave this class having just memorized a sheet of algorithms, you're soon going to find yourself in deep trouble.

In order to handle novel problems, it is important to understand how an algorithm works and how it can be adapted to new problems. The basic idea behind binary search—using the structure in the data to repeatedly halve the search space—is more important than the details of a particular application. Using that one piece of intuition, you can adapt binary search to search circular (but still sorted) arrays or even determine the optimal temperature for your coffee, by testing warmer and cooler coffee until it's "just right."

Socks: An Interlude and an Introduction

Chaos erupted on the deck as the thugs danced away from the wash of pickling juices and sliding eels. A second barrel landed a moment later, sending out a fresh wave. The eels, Deepwater Longbacks by the look of them, measured around four feet from end to end and threatened to trip and tangle, not to mention disgust. A group of three thugs fell into a heap as they tried to escape the splash zone.

Frank jumped to his feet, grabbed Notation's arm, and yanked her up.

"What's going on?" she shouted as a third barrel sailed over their heads and hit the railing.

"No idea," said Frank. "But now's our chance. This way!"

He pulled Notation toward the railing at the ship's edge, sliding through the puddles of pickling juices and piles of eels. A fourth barrel hit the deck and sent the thugs scurrying again. The deck was beginning to look like a grotesque bowl heaped with long, pale gray noodles.

Alongside the ship bobbed a small, nondescript, but oddly familiar schooner loaded with more barrels. A teenage boy, dressed in wizard's robes, was rolling a new barrel onto a contraption composed of planks.

"We should jump for it," said Notation.

"Jump," agreed Frank, eyeing the other ship. He didn't recognize the boy but figured that he must be an enemy of the Vinettees. Nobody in their right mind would fling pickled eels at the Vinettees unless they were already at war. Then again, very few people in their right mind would chose eels as a weapon under any circumstance.

Notation nodded, pulled herself onto the railing, and jumped without hesitation. She sailed through the air, clearing the gap easily, and landed on the schooner's deck.

Frank pulled himself up onto the railing, muttered a handful of Boolean curse words, and hesitated again as he balanced on the wooden beam. Then, after counting to three a few times, he jumped. Frank missed the schooner by two feet and plunged into the freezing water. He surfaced in time to see another barrel soar overhead. He paused briefly to wonder if the boy was still flinging eels or whether he had moved onto something else—soft cheeses, perhaps.

Notation reached down and pulled him onto the ship. He got to his feet and began wringing out his cloak while he assessed their new situation. The teenager was continuing his barrage of the *Retry Loop*. Sailors hurried around the deck, pushing the smaller ship away from the *Retry Loop* with long wooden poles.

"Mavis?" Frank called loudly. "I know you're here somewhere."

Mavis appeared a second later from the hold. "He paid for the cargo," she said, pointing at the teenager. "It's up to him how he wants to unload it."

"I thought you couldn't—"

Mavis waved him off. "I owed the Vinettees one anyway," she explained. "Last month they stole one of my caches—17 bushels of carrots!"

Frank stared at her in amazement. Going against the Vinettees was dangerous business. A hundred bushels of carrots wouldn't be close to worth it.

"Don't look at me like that, Frank," she said. "I'm not doing this out of the goodness of my heart. It's a paid contract. Simple as that. Socks made it worth my while."

"Socks?" asked Frank.

"Socks?" asked Notation.

Mavis motioned toward the boy, then shrugged. "That's what he called himself. In my business, you don't press for real names."

"You didn't ask for official identification before letting him board?" asked Notation. Mavis gave her a skeptical look.

By now, Mavis's crew had gotten the *TCP Flyer* turned around, and they were heading out to sea. Dirty sails were hoisted into the air, blocking Socks's barrel throwing. He took a last long look at the *Retry Loop*, smiled, and turned finally to Frank.

"Hi," he said with all too much cheerfulness, "I'm Socks." He held out his hand. Frank shook it warily.

"Thank you for saving us, *Socks*," Notation said as she shook his hand too. She eyed him beadily, then, apparently unsatisfied with the subtlety of her approach, followed with, "What's your real name, Socks?"

"Unfortunately, that is my real name," replied Socks a little sadly. "My full name is Socks Repellent, Officer."

"Oh . . . " Notation trailed off. Evidently failing to find any suitable consolation for such a misfortune, she repeated, "Thank you for saving us."

"Anytime," replied Socks. "I didn't have any experience flinging barrels, so I'm glad it worked."

"Why did you help us, Socks?" Frank asked. "More importantly, how did you know we needed help?"

"Well," said Socks. "You see . . . I've been following you both all morning."

"The alley on Three Bit Lane?" asked Frank.

"Yes," replied Socks, blushing. "And behind the big ArrayCart in parking space #2."

"I missed that one," Frank admitted.

"His legs were clearly visible by the wheels," said Notation.

"Why were you following me?" asked Frank.

"Us," corrected Notation.

"Because we're after the same people," said Socks as though it were the most obvious answer in the world.

"We are?" asked Notation.

"I think so," said Socks, suddenly looking uncertain. "You're investigating one of the police department thefts, right? I saw Captain Donovan visit Frank last night, so I assumed it had something to do with the one at headquarters."

"*Thefts?*" asked Frank. "There's been more than one?"

"Oh," said Socks. "You didn't know. Sorry. Maybe I wasn't supposed to say anything. But I don't think that was supposed to be secret. I guess—"

"Why are the wizards concerned about thefts from police stations?" Frank cut in.

"The king called them in. A few weeks ago, King Fredrick summoned some of the kingdom's most senior and respected wizards to investigate a theft. I'm Gretchen's apprentice, of course. It's only my second year, but—"

"Why did he call in senior wizards?" Frank interrupted again. Gretchen wasn't a name he'd heard before. Evidently, the more powerful wizards had been occupied with more pressing tasks, and the king had worked his way down the list, but Frank didn't want to embarrass the boy by questioning his mentor's seniority.

"The Capital Police are well equipped to handle thefts," added Notation. "It should be their investigation."

"The king called in the wizards to consult about the mask and whether they could find it," explained Socks.

"What mask?" asked Notation.

"You don't know about the mask?" said Socks, now a little panicked. "Oh, dear. Maybe I shouldn't have said anything."

"What mask?" growled Frank. He rubbed his temples and took a few deep breaths.

"Mr. Repellent," took up Notation in her official police voice, "we are on an important investigation. If you have information that would help in this case, it is your duty to provide it. Please tell us everything."

"Start at the beginning," added Frank.

It took 10 minutes for Socks to finish his excessively detailed story concerning a monthlong crime spree in which a multitude of unrelated items were stolen from secure locations. The most disturbing revelation involved the theft of a dangerous magical artifact, an enchanted mask, from a military convoy. When pressed for details on what the mask did or why it needed an armed escort, Socks would only repeat that it was "extremely powerful." The awe in his voice made Frank nervous.

"You think this theft is related to the one at the police station?" asked Notation.

"Gretchen thinks so," Socks answered. "In every case, the guards were completely unaware that a theft had occurred until the next day. She thinks the thief used a memory spell or a sleep charm."

"I did not fall asleep," Notation said with such force that even Frank leaned away.

"I . . . I didn't mean," Socks stammered.

Frank left him to flail about for words as he pondered the kid's story. Something about it didn't add up. "Why tail us?" he asked finally. "You're on an investigation sanctioned by the king himself, right? You could have just walked up and introduced yourself."

"Yes! But . . . " Socks trailed off.

"But?" asked Frank.

"I wasn't sure it would be worthwhile," admitted Socks.

Frank glared at him until he continued.

"I wasn't sure you were going to find anything interesting," explained Socks. "Once I introduced myself, I would be obliged to come with you and help out, right? I wanted to keep my options open. What if I heard about a better, magical lead or something? Sorry," the boy muttered.

They lapsed into thoughtful silence as the ship's crew continued to dash around them, doing whatever was needed to make a ship move. As far as Frank could tell, it seemed to primarily involve pulling on ropes.

"So . . . what now?" asked Socks.

"We follow leads," said Frank.

"We found two suspicious ports in the *Retry Loop*'s logs," Notation explained. "Our next step is to investigate them, starting with the Port of Mudwall. In fact, I should inform the captain of the ship. Of course, we'll need to borrow her vessel for the investigation."

Frank laughed. "Good luck explaining that to Mavis."

"No need," said Socks hurriedly. "I already paid to contract the ship. You just need to tell Mavis where to sail."

"Excellent," said Notation.

"Which means you're coming with us, doesn't it?" asked Frank, without trying to conceal the irritation in his voice.

"Of course," said Socks. "I paid for the ship. And I saved you. And I seem to know more about the case than anyone else here. And I'm an apprentice wizard. That could come in handy." His desperation seemed to increase with every additional reason.

"Mr. Repellent, we would be grateful for your assistance," Notation assured him. "Wouldn't we, Frank?"

"Yeah. Great," mumbled Frank. He had collected yet another tagalong whom he didn't trust. At this rate, he would have a boatful by nightfall.

— 9 —
Backtracking to Keep the Search Going

The Port of Mudwall didn't even live up to its unimpressive name. It wasn't much of a port; the rickety wooden dock could fit no more than two modestly sized ships. The mudwall itself, in theory a 20-foot-tall earthen city wall, had never actually been constructed, and was only hinted at here and there with 2-foot-tall humps surrounding about a third of the city.

Frank stepped over the dirt hump and made his way to the sole shop in the city, with Notation and Socks trailing along behind him.

As they entered the store, the shopkeeper's face transformed from surprise to outright delight with the progression of a powerful sneeze. He knocked a stack of carrot-themed tourist pamphlets off the counter as he hurried around to greet them.

"Hello!" he nearly shouted. "Welcome to Mudwall, home of the famous mud carrot farms. What can I get for you? Food? Supplies? Carrots? Carrot-flavored baked goods? We have a simply wonderful carrot pie."

"Information," said Frank.

The shopkeeper's face dropped. "Oh," he said. "You're not here for the Carrot Festival, then?"

"Carrot Festival?" asked Notation.

The shopkeeper nodded. "It's the 50th annual Carrot Festival later this week."

"You get a lot of visitors for that?" she asked.

"Not recently," admitted the shopkeeper. "Mudwall isn't the tourist draw that it used to be. Not since G'Raph started hosting its Mud Radish Festival. People would rather go there for the big-city atmosphere."

Notation and Socks looked at each other. Socks mouthed, "What's a mud radish?" Notation shrugged.

"What do you know about a ship that came through here a few days ago?" Frank asked.

"What ship?" asked the shopkeeper. "We haven't had a ship here in a few months. We've had a few donkey carts pass through on the coastal road. But no ships."

"Are you sure?" asked Notation. "Because we are on an official investigation, and it is very important that you tell us anything you might know about all ships that have come through here recently."

"I would have known if there was a ship," said the shopkeeper. "I have a wonderful view of the dock from my window. Even if I hadn't seen it, I would have heard about it. We don't get many ships these days. People would've been all excited. The Sound of Carrots, our three-person marching band, usually greets each ship. I certainly would have heard them."

Notation looked as though she was preparing for a new round of questions, but Frank cut in first. "Thank you, sir," he said. "We appreciate your time."

He herded Notation and Socks from the building and back into the muddy street.

"Do you think he was telling the truth?" asked Notation.

Frank nodded, scanning the street. "He seemed genuinely surprised at the mention of a ship," he said. "But it wouldn't hurt to ask around a bit more."

They interviewed a dozen of the town's residents, a sample that made up approximately half the population, before admitting defeat. No one had seen a ship. No one had heard of anyone seeing a ship. And no one could even understand why a ship would visit. The port clearly didn't receive much traffic.

"Maybe it came at night," mused Notation as they walked the dock toward the *TCP Flyer*. "They sent a small party ashore on a rowboat, handed off the documents, and left. Someone could have been waiting with a cart right here." She pointed to an arbitrary plank on the dock, which didn't look any more or less suspicious than its neighbors.

"Maybe," said Frank. "It doesn't matter, though. Without a witness, there's no trail."

"What does that mean? We can't find them? The investigation is over?" asked Socks.

Frank grunted a laugh. "No, kid. Dead ends are part of investigation work. That's why we use a backtracking search."

Socks stared blankly back at Frank. When comprehension failed to dawn on the boy's face, Frank added, "We keep exploring along the most promising direction until that trail hits a dead end. Then we backtrack to a previously unexplored, but promising, lead and search from there."

"So you have other leads?" asked Socks.

"A few," admitted Frank.

"If we backtrack to the next unexplored clue," Notation mused, "we return to the logbook. There was another destination listed: Frayed Cable Island."

Frank nodded and considered which leads remained. The senior thug had mentioned a League of something. That meant Frank's pitiful list of unexplored leads currently consisted of:

> Frayed Cable Island
> Threads from the ArrayCart
> Vinettees
> League?

The search would now backtrack to the logbook and the unexplored island. If they failed to pick up a trail on Frayed Cable Island, he would be forced to follow one of their more tenuous leads. The colored threads from the cart were unique enough to be moderately promising.

"So we aren't done yet?" Socks confirmed for the tenth time as the *TCP Flyer* traveled to Frayed Cable Island. "You still have a few leads, right?"

"Investigations backtrack all the time," Notation assured him yet again. "Don't you ever have to backtrack in your work? What about while making a potion?"

Socks looked shocked. "How would you backtrack while mixing a potion? You can't unadd spider legs or unstir the mixture."

"I meant backtrack while *developing* a potion. You try adding spider legs and realize that it destroys the magical consistency or something? So you cross out that instruction and try a different approach the next time you mix the potion. Each recipe you try is a single state in your search space, and you backtrack by returning to the last good recipe."

"Oh," said Socks. "You mean *revising*. You have to revise spells and potions as you develop them. You're still moving toward your goal, just not in a straight line. Nobody gets it right the first time."

"Exactly. It's the same thing," said Notation.

Mavis joined the group, adding, "It's like when you're searching a cave for a 'forgotten' stash of goods, you explore down different paths and backtrack when you don't see anything of value."

"Yes," Notation agreed, hestitantly. "Backtracking search is much like exploring caves. Although I have to point out that it would be difficult to tell if an object found was forgotten or not. I guess you could—"

"And speaking of searches, we're at your next destination," interrupted Mavis. "Frayed Cable Island doesn't have any docks. We'll anchor the *TCP Flyer* here, but you lot will have to row in the rest of the way."

POLICE ALGORITHMS **101**: BACKTRACKING
Excerpt from Professor Drecker's Lecture

Almost every investigation will involve some backtracking. Even the best officers can't always follow clues in a straight path from start to finish. The world is filled with useless information, ambigious clues, and red herrings. On top of that, you'll make mistakes. So it's important to know how to backtrack a search when you hit a dead end. Simply put, this means backing up your search to a previous state and trying a different option.

continued

Up until this point, algorithms have been presented on search spaces where they can efficiently jump from any state to any other arbitrary state. For example, in an array, you can easily examine the value at any location using just its index. And in a hotel hallway, you can run between rooms. This flexibility provides efficiency for the algorithms.

However, many search spaces come with constraints on how you can move from state to state. If you are searching a castle in the physical world, you can't jump arbitrarily between rooms—you have to traverse the halls and rooms in between. Similar constraints can apply in the computational realm for data structures like graphs or linked lists.

Even in cases where you can jump between states, it is often useful to picture backtracking as moving through previous states on your way to explore new states. In the algorithmic world, this can be significantly less costly than physically retracing your route. However, the processes are conceptually similar: you back up the search and proceed down a different avenue.

In the following lectures, we'll see many examples of searches that backtrack when they hit dead ends. And once you join the force, you'll experience more dead ends than you ever imagined.

Picking Locks with Breadth-First Search

Frank, Socks, and Officer Notation huddled by the back gate of the prison's outer wall. Despite its truly impressive coating of rust, the locked gate had resisted both of Frank's attempts to kick it open. He had only succeeded in clouding the air with red dust and introducing Notation to at least six new Boolean curse words.

"So . . . that didn't work," supplied Socks. Frank ignored him and studied the locking mechanism. It was a standard carved keypad with buttons labeled 1, 2, 3, A, B, and C in a single ordered row and an ENTER button beneath.

"We'll have to do this the old-fashioned way," said Frank.

"Wasn't kicking down the gate the old-fashioned way?" asked Notation.

Frank ignored her as well. "Socks, do you know any magic lock-picking spells?"

"No," Socks protested loudly. "Those are illegal!"

"How about something to weaken the lock? Or maybe the hinges?" asked Frank.

"You want me to help you destroy property?" Socks looked aghast. "That's worse than lock picking. Do you know how much trouble—"

"Search spells, then? The Spell of All Combinations or the Spell of Breadth-First Search?" Notation interrupted. She'd heard enough on the topic of proper and improper spellwork after Frank had casually inquired about the feasibility of replication spells on gold coins—a use of magic that fell firmly on the wrong side of both Socks's and her own ethical line.

"I've used the Spell of Breadth-First Search a few times," Socks answered. "My real expertise is binary search trees, but I'm familiar with a range of computational techniques. Once I—"

"Will breadth-first search work on the lock?" interrupted Frank. Over the years, Frank had worked cases with a handful of wizards of varying levels of respectability. He'd seen at least a dozen different lock-picking spells but had never seen a door opened with an explicit breadth-first search.

Notation smiled. "Definitely! It's a bit abstract, but I saw a similar problem recently in my Police Algorithms course. When you think about it, a code lock is just a search problem; you enter a string of characters to open it. The search space is all possible strings that can be made from those characters. Every string is a valid search option, from a single character like 1 or A to complex sequences like ABC123CBA321. The search target is the one string that opens the lock."

"But we don't even know how many characters we need," protested Socks. "The lock could have a 30-character combination."

"That's why she suggested breadth-first search," said Frank, thinking aloud as much as addressing Socks's concern.

"I don't understand," said Socks.

Notation quickly picked up the explanation. "You see, breadth-first search expands outward from a starting point, exploring along a frontier of solutions. Naturally it will try the shorter solutions first."

"Huh?" asked Socks, now looking confused to the point of panic. "I thought breadth-first search used magic lists. I've always used a magic list. Isn't it just a magic list?"

"Yes," agreed Notation. "Breadth-first search maintains a list of options to try next if the current option doesn't work. The algorithm is basically a loop that keeps pulling options from the front of the list and adding new options to the back. On each iteration, we pick a new option to try from the *front* of the list. And, if that's not what we want, we check if there are any new options reachable from the current one and add those unexplored options to the *back* of the list.

"You start at a single point in the search space, in this case at a password of length zero. Then for each password you try, you add new search possibilities to the end of the list. In this case, each time we try a password, we'll add all single-character extensions to the list. For example, here we know the password can only contain the characters 1, 2, 3 and A, B, and C. Once we've tested 3A, we'll add 3A1, 3A2, 3A3, 3AA, 3AB, and 3AC to the end of our list."

Socks screwed his face up in concentration, then asked, "How do we know which options to add?"

"Think of it like a tree of possibilities," suggested Notation. "Each branch, or *node*, is a password from our list, like 3A. The neighboring options are the nodes under it—the passwords we would get by adding one more character to the end. Breadth-first search progresses down each level of the tree before moving onto the next."

"Since we add the new, longer passwords to the *end* of our list, we try all the short stuff first," Frank threw in. "Now, can you do it?"

"This isn't a proper use of—"

"Come on! Really?" interrupted Frank.

"It's basically a lock-picking spell," responded Socks.

"Yes. That's exactly what it is!" shouted Frank.

"Forget it," said Notation, throwing her arms up in frustration. "If he doesn't feel comfortable picking the lock, we're not going to change his mind by yelling." She turned and studied the stone wall itself, which stood at least 10 feet tall. After a moment she continued, "Frank, if you give me a boost, maybe I can climb over."

Frank gave the wall a skeptical look. Despite having been abandoned for years, the wall lacked the large cracks and rambling vines that often aid mountaineering efforts on old castle walls. The workmanship was impressive. Someone had taken real pride in building this wall; you could tell from the artistic way the metal spikes twisted as they jutted up. Those little details took effort.

"Maybe. It's pretty high, though, and those spikes look awfully sharp," he said.

"It'll be just like the obstacle course at the academy," said Notation. "Aside from the hard-packed ground, the lack of handholds, and the large metal spikes, that is."

"Those'll probably add some excitement," Frank offered.

"Shut up and give me a boost, Frank."

"No. No. I'll do it," said Socks hurriedly. "I'll use the Spell of Breadth-First Search. I'll need something for the list, though. A roll of parchment, perhaps?"

Frank and Notation looked at each other. "No can do, kid. Use the ground; it's muddy enough."

"Oh. Yes. Of course."

A few minutes later, the lock began to glow. "Here we go," said Socks.

The word ENTER glowed briefly, followed by a clicking noise. But the gate remained locked. The spell had tried the first password, which was nothing at all. Next a series of numbers and letters appeared in the mud:

1, 2, 3, A, B, C

Frank could picture the tree of possible passwords that the list represented.

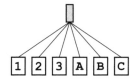

An instant later, the number 1 glowed, followed by ENTER. Again the gate clicked, but didn't open. The list on the ground changed, showing the new list of passwords to try, branching out to the third level of the tree.

2, 3, A, B, C

11, 12, 13, 1A, 1B, 1C

But these were added to the end of the list. The search itself continued on the current level, trying 2.

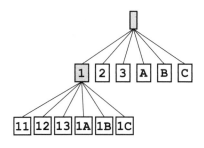

The password 2 didn't work, and the list grew again.

3, A, B, C

11, 12, 13, 1A, 1B, 1C

21, 22, 23, 2A, 2B, 2C

Again the tree branched out with new possibilities, but the search still worked its way along the current level, trying all one-character passwords before moving deeper.

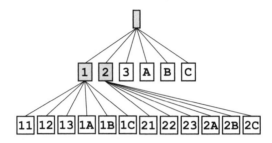

In other words, the search explored the full breadth of each level before moving on to deeper levels.

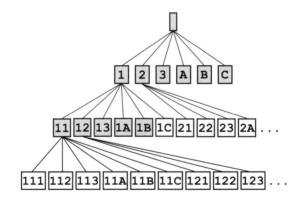

The search finished the first level, trying the passwords 3, A, B, and C, before Socks broke the silence. "This could take a while."

Frank nodded, eyes fixed on the ever-growing list of numbers. "Notation, why don't you scout around the front?"

"Okay," she agreed, her expression betraying great relief. Rookies didn't tend to handle stakeouts well. Sitting still for hours on end with nothing to do wasn't something you could teach at the academy, although Professor Cloud's Philosophy of Law Enforcement lectures came close.

Five minutes after Notation left, the lock gave a loud click, and the gate swung open noisily on its well-rusted hinges. The list in the mud faded as the search algorithm completed.

"1111," said Frank, without a trace of surprise. It often paid to keep the codes simple enough for the henchmen to remember.

He used a stick to write the code in a patch of mud and circled it twice. Even a rookie couldn't miss the message. Then he turned to Socks. "Let's go."

POLICE ALGORITHMS 101:
BREADTH-FIRST SEARCH
Excerpt from Professor Drecker's Lecture

Breadth-first search is an algorithm that explores search states in the order in which they are encountered. In other words, it always attempts to explore the oldest unsearched state first.

You can visualize breadth-first search as keeping a list (or, more formally, a *queue*) of known but unexplored states. At each step, the algorithm picks the next state to explore from the front of the queue. As the algorithm discovers new options, it adds them to the back of the queue, to make sure all previous options are explored before it moves on to new options.

It's helpful to describe breadth-first search in terms of how it explores a graph. A graph is a data structure composed of

continued

individual *nodes*, with *edges* linking those nodes. If two nodes are connected by an edge, we say they are *neighbors*, which means you can move between those nodes. During your orientation, you studied at least one graph—the Kingdom Highway Map. This map represents each city as a node and the highways connecting them as edges. Make sure you own a good copy of that map. Criminals have a tendency to flee the city, and you'll need to know to which neighboring cities they are most likely to go.

Searching the Kingdom Highway Map is a classic graph search problem. Our search states are the nodes of the graph—the cities on the map. Imagine that a crime has occurred in city A and it is your job to find the fleeing criminal.

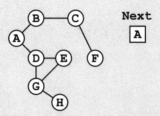

Breadth-first search explores along an expanding frontier, checking each node X steps away from the initial node before proceeding to any nodes $X + 1$ steps away. After you explore city A, its two neighbors, B and D, are added to the back of the queue. No other cities were in the queue, so B is the next city you'll visit.

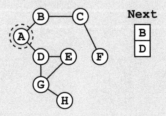

If each node has many neighbors, maintaining the queue of nodes to explore can use a large amount of memory. This memory requirement can become expensive in large search problems. As an officer, you'll want to invest in a number of good notebooks.

At each step in breadth-first search, we test whether the current node is the target node. In this example, that means thoroughly checking the city for our criminal. If the current node isn't the target node, we add only its previously unseen neighbors to the list. (A node that is *unseen* hasn't been added to the list yet.) We thus avoid adding either nodes that we have already explored or unexplored nodes that are already on our list. In this case, for instance, after checking city B, we would not add A to our list again.

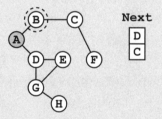

Note that checking whether a neighbor is unseen requires even more memory because we must keep track of previously seen nodes. However, the benefit is significant—we avoid loops through previously explored nodes. Again, carefully keeping track of your search can pay off significantly.

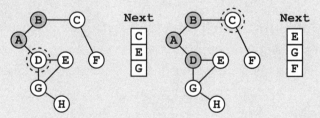

continued

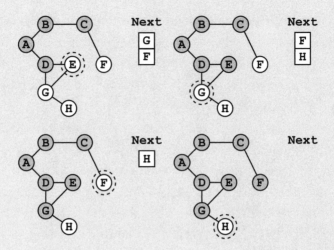

In this particular example, we find our suspect hiding in city H. We can stop our search there and make the arrest.

In search problems where moving between any two neighboring nodes has the same cost (time, energy, etc.), breadth-first search is guaranteed to find a path with the least total cost. It accomplishes this by expanding outward from the starting node, exploring *every* node that is X steps away before exploring any state that is $X + 1$ steps away.

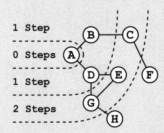

Breadth-first search can even be adapted to return the shortest path by keeping *back pointers*. Each node keeps track of the node that preceded it. Then, upon finding the goal state, you can trace the pointers backward to re-create the path.

However, keep in mind that this works only if each move between neighbors has the same cost. In the general case, minimizing the number of steps in the search space can be very different from minimizing the cost of the path to the goal. For example, if hikers want to minimize their energy expended (cost), they would prefer a longer route that avoids crossing a mountain range. While the mountain pass would be shorter, and arguably more scenic, it could require significantly more energy.

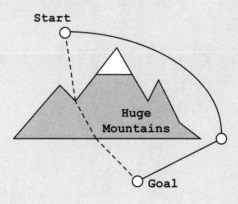

Depth-First Search in an Abandoned Prison

Two steps into the prison, and Frank knew they had walked into a maze. The old computational prisons used to rely on their bizarre structure as much as on guards. Potential escapees think twice about sneaking through a door when they don't know what lies on the other side: freedom or the guard's breakroom.

"How about some light?" suggested Frank.

"Oh. Right," agreed Socks. He muttered an incantation and a bluish flame flickered from the end of his staff, lighting up the completely unremarkable room.

The square room, rough stone walls, and heavy oaken door were enough to confirm what Frank already knew: the entire structure was a grid of rooms, each with doors to only some of its neighbors. They would have to navigate from room to room. But since they didn't know which rooms had doors between them, they would have to search out a path as they went.

"Time for another search," he said.

"A search?" asked Socks. "For what?"

"The papers, of course," responded Frank. He had no doubt that the papers were stashed here. An abandoned prison provided an ideal location for stashing stolen goods, clearly surpassing the more commonly used warehouse. Arguably, the only better location would be an abandoned castle—provided it had a moat. The question now was whether they could find the documents and then, if they did, whether the documents would provide any valuable clues.

"Not another breadth-first search," protested Socks.

Frank considered the idea. In theory, breadth-first worked fine on a grid. Each state of the search space was a grid square. Once you explored one grid square, you could add its unexplored neighboring squares to your list of things to try. Frank could clearly picture the search propagating out over an empty grid, like a wave moving across the water.

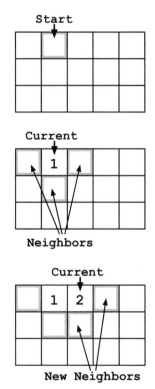

However, breadth-first search had one major drawback in the physical world—an excessive amount of backtracking. Since you were always adding items to the end of the list, the next square to explore could be annoyingly far away. Even on an empty grid, without walls blocking your path, you could find yourself hiking back to the other end of the search space.

It was the type of unnecessary movement that Frank made it a policy to avoid.

"No," said Frank. "Too much backtracking. We're better off going depth-first here."

"Depth-first search. Depth-first search," Socks mumbled to himself as though willing the spell into his memory. "I—I don't think I remember—"

Frank waved him off, and strode confidently down the corridor. "We don't need a spell for this one. I've been doing depth-first searches through buildings since you were in diapers."

"No backtracking with depth-first search then?" asked Socks.

"There's backtracking with most search algorithms. But backtracking in a depth-first search is better suited for walking."

"Um . . . I see."

"No, you don't," said Frank bluntly. "If you don't know the algorithm, just ask. Pretending to know algorithms is a recipe for disaster. I've seen too many rookies tripped up due to bad searches. Good kids, like you."

"Okay. What is depth-first search?" Socks asked.

"It's a simple algorithm," explained Frank. "Basically we explore deeply down each path. We go down one path until we hit a dead end. Then we backtrack to the most recent path that we didn't take and try that. We'll stop when we find the target.

"In this case, we're going to use clockwise ordering. Whenever we have multiple options, we'll try north, east, south, then west—avoiding paths we've already tried, of course. We'll use the same ordering at every intersection, so we'll always prefer going north if we can. But in this case we have only one option, so we start by going south."

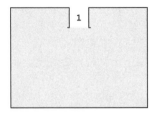

Even as Frank spoke, they reached their first decision point. Frank surveyed the options. They had come from the north, so he chose east—the next unexplored direction in his ordering. Before leaving the intersection, he retrieved a piece of chalk from his pocket and made a small mark on the wall.

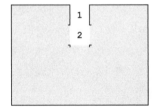

After two more intersections—turning north, then east—they reached their first dead end. So far the rooms had either been completely empty or contained only the odd prison cell—the cells being enclosures within the rooms. With the complete lack of other distinguishing characteristics, Frank chalked a number onto a wall in each room and linked that number in his mind to the different mold formations he found there.

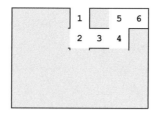

"Now we backtrack to the last room, room 5, with the mold that looked like a horse," explained Frank as they retraced their steps. This time they chose the only unexplored option from room 5, heading west. Unfortunately, they immediately hit another dead end—an empty room that sported a complex floral pattern of green and blue fuzz.

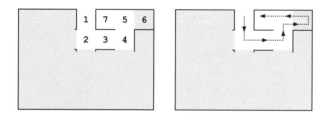

They backtracked through the most recent intersection whose options had been exhausted until they had a new option at room 4. The eastern option was a dead end, and they'd already explored the northern option, so this time they went south.

They ventured through two new empty rooms (8 and 9), differentiated only by the occurrence of a large stalactite of orange mold, which they stayed as far away from as possible. Orange mold was not known for its structural stability. After hitting another dead end, they found themselves retracing their steps all the way back to the first intersection in room 2.

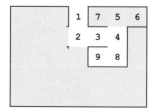

"What if we miss it?" asked Socks in his now-standard worried tone. "Or what if we end up in a loop? We could be stuck forever!"

Frank groaned. "Listen, kid. This isn't my first time depth-first searching. I know what I'm doing."

"But loops."

"Why do you think I'm marking the walls?" asked Frank. "If we avoid taking passages that we've already explored, we avoid going in loops."

Frank had learned that lesson during a Police Algorithms exercise. With the whole class watching, Frank had done six loops of the hedge maze before he heard another student loudly joke, "There he goes again."

They explored deeper into the maze, following snaking paths and backtracking at dead ends.

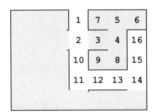 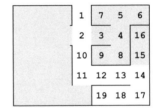

Then, in room 23, they found a small cell packed high with rolls of parchment and stacks of ledgers.

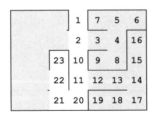 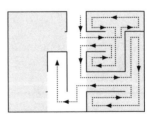

"We found it!" said Socks enthusiastically. His staff's flame cast a flickering blue glow through the room.

Frank felt the hairs on his neck rise as he took in the scene. He compared the height of the stacks with the mountains of paperwork he had completed through the years and did some quick calculations. The captain had never been shy about dumping paperwork on him, but Frank had still never seen anything like this. There were even mold-stained pages at the bottom of the stacks. Everything felt wrong.

Frank walked to the nearest stack and pulled off a sheet of parchment: a notice on the proper use of duck fences. The date and station number marked it as belonging to the stolen files. The next sheet, listing noise complaints in the Port of West Serial, also came from the stolen collection. It appeared equally random and unhelpful.

He knelt down and pried open a gap near the bottom, yanking a ledger free. The pages were spotted with a trio of mold-butterflies, but Frank could clearly make out supply lists for the castle guards. This ledger could have come only from the castle itself. He grabbed another book and found castle guard rotations for last November.

"This is wrong," he muttered. "There's too much here. There's castle ledgers as well." Frank shifted to an adjacent pile, starting again at the top.

"Is there a pattern?" asked Socks, as though he had just noticed the extent of the document piles.

"I—" started Frank, but he pulled up short as he opened another ledger, entitled *Transfer Requests*. Four pages had been torn from the middle of the ledger.

"Very strange," said Frank, flipping through the undamaged pages. "This could be—"

Frank was cut off as Socks stumbled toward him, flailing for balance. Behind him, Frank could see motion in the gloom. It wasn't until he heard the rusty shriek of the door's hinges that he realized what was happening.

"Door!" Frank yelled as the junior wizard fell into him.

The two of them tumbled to the ground. The door slammed. A loud click sounded as the lock engaged. Socks's staff, which had been dropped in the commotion, spun lazily into a tall stack of dry parchment. The staff's blue flame seemed much larger than Frank remembered.

Frank lay stunned on the stone floor as he watched the papers ignite.

POLICE ALGORITHMS 101:
DEPTH-FIRST SEARCH
Excerpt from Professor Drecker's Lecture

Unlike breadth-first search, depth-first search is an algorithm that explores more recently encountered search states first. The algorithm progresses down paths until it hits either the target or a dead end.

As with breadth-first search, you can visualize depth-first search as keeping a list (in this case, a *stack*) of known but unexplored states. At each step, the algorithm picks the next state to explore from the top of the stack. But unlike breadth-first search, depth-first search adds new options to the *top* of the stack.

Consider our graph example from the lecture on breadth-first search. Remember, graphs are data structures composed of individual nodes and edges linking those nodes. They can be used to represent all sorts of concepts, like city maps, networks of criminals, or even the layout of a castle. We'll use the Kingdom Highway Map from the same lecture and start our search from city A—the scene of the crime.

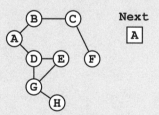

Depth-first search explores down one path until it hits a dead end (or a node it has already explored). In this way, the algorithm prioritizes exploring *deeply* down paths over exploring *broadly* over the options, as in breadth-first search.

continued

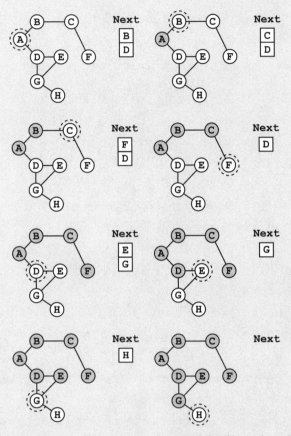

Once again, we find our suspect hiding in city H—although this time we travel a different path during our search.

As with breadth-first search, we avoid exploring nodes more than once by keeping track of previously visited nodes. This check is particularly important if you want to avoid falling into endless loops, checking the same nodes over and over again. In the above example, we avoid adding previously seen nodes (either explored or unexplored) to our list altogether.

Cafeteria Stacks and Queues

Frank pushed himself into a crouch and hurried to the door. He tugged and pulled, rattling and thumping the door against its lock. He grasped the rusted iron bars and threw his full weight into the effort, but succeeded only in producing louder clanking sounds.

Frank turned to Socks, hoping the young wizard knew a bar-bending spell. Given the circumstances, he felt confident that Socks would even consent to using a lock-picking spell. But as Frank's eye caught the smoldering stacks of parchment and the trails of smoke wisping to the ceiling, he froze. An image of a smoke-filled kitchen flashed across his mind, dredging up forgotten memories of his first year in the academy. He could almost hear the cook shouting. Frank shut his eyes hard, trying to force the memory away.

During his first two months at the academy, Frank had balanced his classes with a work-study job in the school cafeteria. The job wasn't anything glamorous; they didn't let new arrivals wash dishes, let alone prepare the food. Instead, Frank spent 15 hours a week transporting loads of clean trays, plates, and cutlery from the kitchen to the appropriate locations in the cafeteria.

Despite the tedious nature of the work, Frank found himself enjoying it. "Look at me! I'm undoing your work. I'm the anti-busboy," he would shout to the trio of busboys clearing tables and filling bins with dirty dishes. He unsuccessfully tried to break the school record for the most number of dishes transported in two minutes. He created an entirely new cafeteria game called Fling the Spoon. But it wasn't until a fortuitous run-in with Professor Heappens that he actually learned something from the job.

"Ugh. There are some data structures that just don't belong in the cafeteria," Professor Heappens muttered loudly as he studied the food options.

At 2:30 in the afternoon, the lunch rush had vanished, and Frank Runtime was hard at work transporting a load of bowls to the soup station. Though the comment wasn't directed at him, he found himself asking the professor, "What data structures?"

"Stacks," Professor Heappens said, looking up at Frank. "Stacks almost never belong in a cafeteria."

"Sure they do," Frank replied with the level of certainty that only new students and the truly ignorant can muster. He nodded down at the stack of bowls he was carrying. "Stacks of bowls. Stacks of plates. Stacks of pancakes."

Professor Heappens made a dismissive gesture and started walking away. "What do you know about data structures anyway?"

"How else are you supposed to arrange plates?" Frank asked. "If you laid them out end to end, they would take too much room."

The professor stopped and stared at Frank with an expression of profound concern. After nearly a minute, he asked, "Do you know the difference between a stack and a queue?"

Frank shook his head. He hadn't taken Police Data Structures yet.

"A stack is a *last-in, first-out* data structure," explained the professor. "It has two operations. You can *push* something onto the top of the stack. Or you can *pop* something off the top of the stack.

He gestured at the stack of plates waiting at the front of the line. "It's just like the stack of plates over there. You can push a plate onto the stack."

He placed his empty plate on top of the stack.

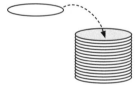

"Or you can pop a plate off the top." He grabbed his plate back.

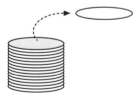

"And whenever you pop something off a stack, you get the newest item on the stack. The oldest item will stay at the bottom of the stack until you have popped off everything above it."

"So?" Frank asked. "What's wrong with that?"

"Nothing's wrong with a last-in, first-out data structure if you use it correctly. Stacks are wonderful if you are writing a depth-first search; you just keep pushing new search options onto the stack and popping them off when you backtrack. But cafeterias have misused stacks for decades!

"Take this stack of plates right here. Do you know how long the bottom plate has been there?"

Frank tried to recall the last time he had seen the stack empty, but couldn't even conjure the image.

"Five years!" shouted Professor Heappens. "I know, because I marked it. For five years that bottom plate has sat there unused, while students like yourself dump other clean plates on top. It sits there collecting dust around the edges.

"But that isn't even the worst. Look at what they are doing to the mashed potatoes!"

Frank glanced over at the large wooden bowl of mashed potatoes. A cook was in the process of refilling it. He held a large pot in one hand and was gleefully ladling fresh mashed potatoes into the bowl. It took a moment for Frank to realize the older food was simply being buried. His stomach turned.

"How long?" he croaked, not really wanting to know the answer.

"Don't worry. They wash out the serving bowl at least once a week, so the old mashed potatoes are less than a week old."

Frank didn't feel reassured. In fact, he felt rather ill. A quick scan of the cafeteria showed the last-in, first-out pattern being utilized everywhere. He stopped when he reached the vats of salad dressing, his stomach roiling with a mixture of nausea and panic.

"What can we do?" he asked.

"Queues," responded the professor. "Queues were practically designed for cafeterias."

"Queues?" asked Frank.

"First-in, first-out data structures," explained Professor Heappens. "Like stacks, they also store things and have two operations. You can *enqueue* something by adding it to the back of the queue. Or you can *dequeue* something by taking it from the front. That way, you are always taking out the oldest item."

Frank tried to picture always taking the bottom plate from a stack. "But how?"

"That's just how the data structure works. Look at the sandwich line; it's a queue. Right now it has four people in it, and the person at the front has been waiting the longest."

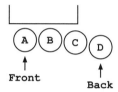

Even as Professor Heappens said that, another person joined the line. "See, they enqueue at the back!" he noted.

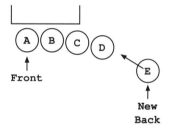

They stood watching the line until the person at the front received her sandwich and departed.

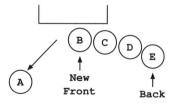

"And dequeue at the front," said the professor happily. "What this cafeteria needs is more queues. Every cafeteria needs more queues."

Frank thought back to the mashed potato stack and realized the professor was right. How the data was stored could have a significant impact on how it was accessed. In cases like mashed potatoes, order mattered.

Despite the seemingly simple revelation, Frank struggled for days to integrate queues into the cafeteria. The plates and bowls were relatively easy. He would simply lift the old pile up and slide new plates underneath. Convincing the cooks to change how they ladled food proved more difficult. They thoroughly enjoyed ladling giant spoonfuls of potatoes, smiling as the large gobs smacked down into the bowl. Frank ultimately suggested a two-bowl method where the old potatoes were ladled onto the top of the new bowl. While it wasn't strictly a queue, it preserved all the fun of slopping mashed potatoes, and the old food didn't get buried at the bottom.

Unfortunately, disaster struck when he filled in for a sick baker. Not paying attention to the fact that the bread was baked in batches for a reason, Frank insisted that loading the oven last-in, first-out was unfair to the bread at the back. He devised a rotation scheme that, every 25 seconds, inserted a new loaf, rotated all the loaves in the oven, and removed the oldest loaf.

Frank's attempt at a baking queue might have worked if the oven had two doors, one at the front and one at the back. Unfortunately, the cafeteria used an older, single-door model, which made rotating the loaves in and out extremely difficult. While the constant churn ensured a more consistent cooking time for all loaves, Frank found himself unable to keep up with the schedule. Soon, dense smoke poured from the hearth as the loaves blackened.

As the other cooks dashed to the fire with buckets of water, Frank stared numbly at the charred loaves. A sense of hopeless confusion crept in as he realized that queues might not be the solution to *every* cafeteria problem. He still had a lot to learn about data structures.

POLICE ALGORITHMS 101: STACKS AND QUEUES
Excerpt from Professor Drecker's Lecture

Stacks and queues are two simple structures for storing data. At first glance, both data structures resemble nothing more than lists of values. How these two data structures differ, though, is in how data is inserted or removed.

A stack is a last-in, first-out data structure that operates much like the pile of papers you'll find on every officer's desk. New elements are *pushed* onto the top of the stack, and elements are removed by being *popped* off the top of the stack. If five elements are pushed onto an empty stack in the order 1, 2, 3, 4, 5, they will be popped off in the reverse order, 5, 4, 3, 2, 1. Of course, as soon as your pile of papers is gone, your captain will just give you more paperwork.

You can implement stacks using an array and a single variable to track the index corresponding to the top of the stack. When you push a new element onto the stack, you add it to the next open slot in the array: index = top + 1. You also increment the top index accordingly.

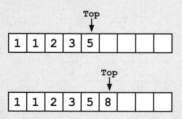

When you pop an element off the stack, you can again use the top index to find the correct element. You can then remove this from the array and decrement the top index accordingly.

continued

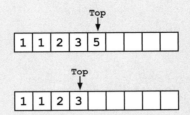

Of course, you must be careful when adding elements to an array of fixed size to avoid going past the end of the array.

A queue is a first-in, first-out data structure, much like a line of suspects waiting to be processed. New elements are *enqueued* at the back of the queue, and elements are removed by being *dequeued* from the front. If five elements are enqueued in an empty queue in the order 1, 2, 3, 4, 5, they will be dequeued in the same order, 1, 2, 3, 4, 5.

Queues can also be implemented with arrays. In this case, you need to track two indexes—the first and last element in the queue. When you enqueue a new element, you add it behind the current last element and increment the back index.

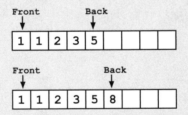

And when you dequeue an element, you remove the front element and increment the front index accordingly.

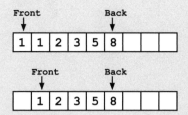

As you enqueue and dequeue elements in a fixed array, a block of empty space will build up at the front of the array. While you can design the queue to wrap, you must take care during both enqueuing and dequeuing to handle indexes being incremented past the end of the array.

Stacks and Queues for Search

Frank shook the image of burnt bread from his mind and returned to the present situation—trapped in a small cell filled with parchment about to burst into flame. The fire was still small, burning the loose sheets at the edge of the piles. But once the large stacks fully caught fire, the heat would be unbearable.

Socks crawled to the door and leaned against it. "Is it locked?" he asked.

Frank swallowed half a dozen snarky answers and simply nodded. "Can you open it?" he asked. "It's an old two-pin lock. It can't have that many combinations."

Socks shook his head. "There's no time. I know a spell to weaken the metal, though. It will ruin the door, but . . . I think that's okay given the circumstances and all."

He retrieved his staff and immediately set to work, mumbling incantations and running his hands over the bars. Spots of rust bloomed under his hands and crept over the metal. Less than a minute later, Socks stood back. The door looked thoroughly rusty, though still very much made of metal.

"The bars should be significantly weakened," he said. He stepped back and gave Frank an expectant look as if to say, "You can smash through the door anytime now."

Frank took a couple of steps back and eyed the door. "How weak?" he asked. "Are we talking toothpick weak or thick plank of wood weak?"

"Well . . . definitely weaker than normal metal," Socks answered. "I added a lot of rust. The bars are thick, but I think they should be pretty weak now."

Frank groaned. He took a deep breath and charged, lowering his shoulder and barrelling into the door. The impact jolted his entire body, but he broke through.

Frank lay sprawled on the floor while a cloudy mixture of rust particles and smoke swirled over him.

Socks hurried over to his side. "Are you okay?" He looked back at the door and broke into a wide smile. "It worked!" he said, beaming with pride. "Were they really weak? What did it feel like?"

"Like inch-thick pine," Frank said. "It hurt a lot."

The smile dimmed slightly. "Oh."

Frank pushed himself to his feet. His shoulder throbbed and he'd have a nasty bruise there tomorrow, but the temporary euphoria of escaping a flaming death easily offset the pain.

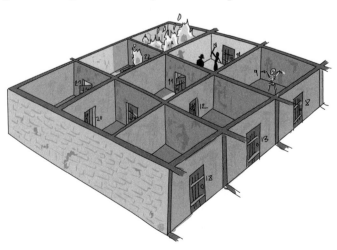

"Time to go," he said as he started through the next room.

"Do you remember how to get back?" Socks asked.

"Of course," Frank replied. "We used depth-first search to get here. We can just follow the stack back out."

"Stack?" Socks asked as he started after Frank.

"Yeah," said Frank, still feeling the lingering thrill of their escape. "It's easy to think of searches in terms of the data structures they use. For example, breadth-first search uses a queue and depth-first search uses a stack." The explanation poured out of him like one of Notation's textbook answers.

"Actually, there are a few different ways to keep track of your options during depth-first search. Some people prefer to use a stack to keep a list of *future* rooms to explore, similar to how you use a queue in breadth-first search. I prefer a different approach.

"You can use the stack to keep track of rooms along your *current* path. Every time you explore a new room, you push it onto a stack representing your current path.

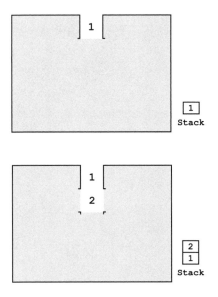

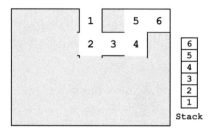

"When you backtrack, you pop that room off the stack and return to the one before it. That way, you always know how to backtrack. I even numbered the rooms to make backtracking easier."

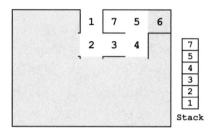

"I thought you always just backtracked to the last decision point," Socks said.

"You effectively do," said Frank. "But keeping the rooms in a stack makes it much easier to do that. You just backtrack and pop off the fully explored rooms until you get to one with a new path."

Socks looked impressed. "You wrote down the rooms we explored?"

"I kept track of the stack in my head and I numbered the rooms with chalk," answer Frank. "As I said, this isn't my first time doing depth-first search. We have to backtrack through seven rooms."

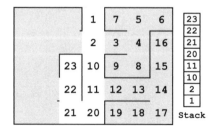

They hurried back through two dark rooms before Socks remembered the staff in his hand. He mumbled the fire incantation again and blue flame leapt from the tip.

Frank eyed the staff warily. "Keep a tight hold of it this time," he advised.

After three more rooms, Socks suddenly asked, "What about queues?"

"What about them?" Frank asked.

"You said they were used for breadth-first search."

"They are," agreed Frank. "Your magic list was just a queue. In *breadth*-first search, the queue tracks the unexplored options. Instead of pushing the current state onto a stack, you add new neighbors to the back of a queue."

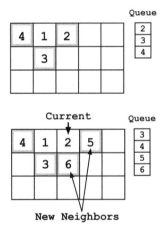

"And in *depth*-first search you can use your list, or stack, to track either the unexplored neighbors or the current path?" asked Socks, rather excitedly for someone fleeing an unknown attacker in an abandoned prison.

"Either approach will work if you're careful about the bookkeeping," agreed Frank.

"I had never thought of search in terms of stacks and queues before," Socks mused. "I wonder what other data structures I'm overlooking. I bet the Spell of Disentangled Ropes uses a few."

Frank ignored his ramblings and continued backtracking to the exit. They moved fast, prioritizing escape over further exploration. Simple logic told Frank that their attacker was long gone. No one had tried to stop them from escaping, and, with the evidence burning, there was nothing for the criminals to gain by waiting around.

Within a few minutes he located the final door, and they rushed outside. A thin trickle of smoke followed them out. By now the flames would have consumed the stacks of paper, destroying any leads.

POLICE ALGORITHMS 101: STACKS AND QUEUES
Excerpt from Professor Drecker's Lecture

The key to efficient algorithms is information. How we organize that information and the data structures we use can have a significant impact not only on the efficiency of the algorithm but also on how the algorithm actually functions. For a simple example of the importance of data structures, consider the breadth-first search and depth-first search from the previous lessons. While the algorithms are conceptually similar, whether we maintain our list of leads in either a stack or a queue significantly changes how the searches progress.

You want to be careful when choosing your data structures. Data structures should help enable the algorithm. Imagine what would happen if we stored a list of sorted numbers in a graph. Even if we maintain the sorted property, we can't perform an efficient binary search over the data because graphs limit how we access the data. Unlike arrays, graphs don't have indexes with which we can access the values. Instead, we are forced to perform a linear scan, moving from one node to the next via the graph's edges.

Let's Split Up: Parallelized Search

W hat happened?" asked Officer Notation, who stood by the gate. Frank studied her as he tried to catch his breath. Was she concerned? Confused?

"We were attacked!" Socks blurted out. "We were trapped in a cell and everything was on fire! But I used a metal weakening spell so we could escape." He looked quite pleased with himself.

"Attacked?" asked Notation. "Who attacked you? Did you see them? What did they look like?"

"No," admitted Socks. "He snuck up behind me."

"Frank?" asked Notation, turning to Frank.

Frank shook his head. "All I saw was Socks flying at me."

"I bet he was big," offered Socks. "A giant thug. And he was stealthy. Maybe a trained assassin."

Frank rolled his eyes. "Sorry, kid. He was an amateur. Professional assassins don't lock people in cells and run away."

"But the fire," said Socks.

"Your staff started the fire," Frank reminded him. "You dropped it on the papers."

"Papers?" asked Notation. "Did you find the logs? Do you know what they were after?"

Frank and Socks looked at each other. Notation glanced from one to the other. Finally, Frank spoke, "The logs are gone. Our junior wizard here dropped his staff and *poof*—fire everywhere. Any clues are gone now."

Socks turned a deep shade of red and stared at the ground.

"Gone?" asked Notation. "Everything's gone? Are you sure?"

"Yeah," said Frank. He nodded toward the smoke trickling from the door.

"What about the person who attacked you?" asked Notation.

"I didn't get a look at him," said Frank. "I don't suppose *you* saw anything?" he asked. The question came out sharper than he'd intended, but after being attacked, getting trapped in a burning room, and fleeing a darkened prison, he didn't feel like pulling any punches.

"No," she said calmly. "There was nothing around the front."

"No tracks near any of the doors?" asked Frank. "Anything that could give us a clue about our attacker?"

Notation shook her head. "Nothing," she said. "It looked as though no one had been around the other side in months."

Frank nodded, but didn't speak. Something felt wrong. Either the attacker had cleverly slipped by Notation through the same gate they had used, or she wasn't telling them something. How long had she been away from the gate? And why had she stayed outside? Frank decided not to press the issue. "All right. Let's head back to the boat."

"Now what?" asked Socks as they made their way toward the water.

"Time to backtrack," said Frank. "No more clues here."

"Backtrack to where?"

"The open clues," Frank answered. "We investigate the leads we still have left." He paused for a moment, weighing his options. "I think it's time we parallelize the search."

"Really?" asked Notation.

"Parallelize?" asked Socks.

"It means we split up and explore different parts of the search space," answered Notation. "Parallel algorithms divide up work and do that work in parallel—at the same time, that is. For example, the work might be distributed over different people. In this case, we can divide the leads into three sets. Then you, Frank, and I can each take a set of leads. We can investigate different leads at the same time, allowing us to work almost three times faster."

"But," objected Socks, "I'm not an officer or a private investigator. I don't know what to do. Shouldn't I stay with one of you?"

"No," said Frank. "I'm still not sure what's going on, but I have a feeling we're working with limited time. Whoever we're after knows we're on the case now and knows we've tracked them this far. If they're smart, they'll start destroying the rest of the evidence."

"It'll be late by the time we get back to Usb," noted Socks.

"We can split up tonight and meet at my office tomorrow morning," said Frank. "That should give us enough time to follow leads and possibly grab some sleep."

"Okay," agreed Notation. "How do we divide up the work?"

Frank knew the key to an efficient parallel algorithm was making sure that the benefit of using multiple workers was worth the cost of dividing up the work. Parallelizing work involves a certain amount of overhead. The problem needs to be broken into pieces. Each worker has to get a task, get ready to do it, and then actually do it. And then at the end, the work has to be recombined. Parallelizing a simple task can sometimes be more costly than just solving it outright. However, when the problem gets large enough, parallelization can greatly accelerate an algorithm.

"Easy," said Frank. "Socks, I need you to talk to your wizard friends. Ask them if they know about a group called the League of something. The thugs on the boat said they were working for a league before Rebecca Vinettee interrupted them. Judging by previous cases, the name will be something evil like the League of

Power-Hungry Maniacs or the League of Darkness. Evil leagues tend not to be subtle with their names. Find out everything you can about this group."

"That's not much to go on," Socks complained.

"Notation," continued Frank. "I need you to pull all police transfer records for the last six months." While he didn't like the idea of leaving this lead to Notation, she was the only one who could get the records easily. If he tried to collect them himself, he would be met with suspicious looks and a small barricade of paperwork. The capital police department used paperwork with the same determination and effectiveness as roadblocks.

"Transfers?" asked Notation, clearly surprised. "Why?"

"Call it a hunch," Frank lied. "We'll meet at my office tomorrow morning and combine our information."

"What about you?" asked Notation. Her voice now carried a note of irritation. She obviously knew Frank wasn't telling her the whole story.

Frank gave her an innocent smile. "I have to go shopping."

As the *TCP Flyer* slowly cruised back to Usb, Frank found an out-of-the-way corner on the deck and sat down to think. This was the part of the investigation he hated most, when promising leads started drying up or, in this case, burning up. The loss of a crucial clue always filled Frank with a sense of dread—like he was running one step behind. Frank forced the doubts from his mind and refocused on the clues he did have. The voyage to Usb would give him time to comb through what he had seen and find connections he had missed.

He closed his eyes and took a deep breath.

"Oh. Sorry. Are you sleeping?" asked Socks.

"No. Thinking," Frank said, and congratulated himself for not yelling. After all, the boy had saved his life.

When Socks didn't say anything more, Frank prompted, "What do you want, Socks?"

"Um . . . I was curious about the search," Socks responded.

"How so?" said Frank.

To Frank's dismay, Socks walked over and sat next to him.

"Do you think we'll find the criminals?" asked Socks.

Frank shrugged. "We've still got some good leads," he offered.

"But do you think we'll be in time?" asked Socks.

Alarm bells went off in Frank's head. He swiveled and stared hard at Socks. "Time for what?"

Socks nearly fell backward. His eyes darted around, as though searching for an appropriate answer. "Whatever they're planning?" he finally stammered.

Frank didn't buy it. "What else do you know?" he asked.

"Nothing," replied Socks. "At least, nothing concrete. It's just speculation. Not mine—my mentor Gretchen's. She has good insight into these types of things, though."

"Which is?"

"I really shouldn't say anything. It's just speculation."

"*Which is?*" Frank growled.

"She thinks that whoever is behind this is going to attack the castle in a few days."

Frank leapt to his feet. "Why didn't you mention this sooner?" he shouted.

"It's just speculation," repeated Socks.

"Unless it is a complete guess, she must have some reason," said Frank. "Is it a guess?"

"No. Not entirely," said Socks. "It's based on the stolen mask. Magical artifacts are most effective during the full moon, which is in two days."

"What exactly does this mask do?" asked Frank, starting to pace anxiously.

Socks hesitated for a moment. "It's an incredibly powerful artifact," he started. Upon seeing the angry look in Frank's eyes, he sped up. "It's officially called the Mask of Combinatorial Looks. It was lost hundreds of years ago during the Great Slug War. Everyone thought it was destroyed until Princess Ann recovered it during one of her quests. She found it—"

"What does it *do*?" prompted Frank.

"It allows the wearer to look like anyone else. The scholars believe that it uses a massively parallel search. Each feature runs its own search to find the best match. The nose will transform into a perfect match of the target's nose. The eyes will transform into—"

"A perfect disguise," offered Frank.

"Yes," said Socks.

Frank cursed. "And the castle? Why does Gretchen think they'll attack the castle?"

"She didn't say," admitted Socks. "Maybe that part *was* a guess," he added without any real conviction.

Frank didn't believe it either.

"I'm sorry I didn't mention it earlier," offered Socks. "Since there isn't any hard proof . . ." He trailed off, looking miserable.

"What else aren't you telling us?" asked Frank, staring down at Socks.

Socks thought about the question for a long while before answering. "I think that's it."

"Everything?"

"Everything I know," Socks qualified.

Frank took a deep breath and looked up at the sails, wishing they were fuller. The wind had died down within the last hour, and the *TCP Flyer* seemed to be barely inching toward their destination.

He ran the timeline of the next few days through his head and wondered if they had enough time. Even with three of them searching in parallel, there was no guarantee they would cover enough ground. Worse, they couldn't even begin the parallel search until the *TCP Flyer* docked. Until then, they were all stuck on the boat.

POLICE ALGORITHMS 101:
PARALLEL ALGORITHMS
Excerpt from Professor Drecker's Lecture

A parallel algorithm breaks up a problem into multiple pieces, performs the computation on those pieces at (approximately) the same time, and then combines the results when all pieces are finished. It divides up the work among different workers, allowing them to complete the task faster than a single worker could. Consider our favorite example: searching an abandoned building for a suspect. The more officers you have, the more rooms you can check at the same time and the faster you can find the suspect.

continued

If you have 30 rooms and 30 officers, they can kick in all the doors at once.

The key to an efficient parallel algorithm is to efficiently divide the work into independent units and then recombine it. Some problems are trivial to parallelize. For example, if you are searching a large stack of scrolls for a particular clue, you can easily divide the work by giving each worker a subset of the scrolls.

However, other algorithms are much more difficult or even impossible to parallelize. Even if you have 100 officers, you can't question a suspect any faster. It's an inherently serial problem. You need to base your next question on the suspect's previous answers. And, perhaps more importantly, a suspect can answer only one question at a time. I've seen eight officers shouting questions at the same time. The interrogation doesn't go any faster.

Another aspect to consider when parallelizing algorithms is whether the efficiency is even worth the overhead. A parallel algorithm requires additional setup time to divide the work, as well as completion time to merge the results back together. Individual tasks have to be assigned to different workers, often requiring some amount of communication. Consider the task of searching an unsorted array with only three values. By the time the setup is complete, a single person could have likely scanned through the array many times over.

Iterative Deepening Can Save Your Life

I know that look," said Mavis. Frank looked up at the *TCP Flyer*'s captain in annoyance. He preferred to brood quietly, and this was the second interruption in 10 minutes.

"What look?" he growled.

"That look," she said, waving in Frank's general direction. "You're questioning your search and wondering if you spent too much time on dead ends."

"Why would I be doing that?" Frank asked.

"I heard what the kid said," Mavis explained. "You're suddenly on a tight timeline, and we have at least another hour before we get back to Usb."

Frank nodded. "If this piece of junk—"

"Hey, now. Just because you're questioning your search doesn't give you a reason to insult my ship."

"Yeah. I suppose," Frank mumbled by way of apology.

He had been running through the leads in his mind, wondering if one of them would have provided quicker answers. He knew the log entries were good leads—as good as he could hope to find in a case like this. But they'd been time-consuming. He'd spent almost a full day traveling between ports on the *TCP Flyer*.

With a grunt, Mavis lowered herself and sat next to Frank. "Iterative deepening?"

Frank shrugged. The thought had occurred to him. Iterative deepening was a cross between a pure depth-first search and a breadth-first search. The algorithm searched in rounds, each round being a depth-first search that was limited to a given path length.

"Never was a fan," Frank admitted. He'd never been able to stomach repeating parts of the search over and over each iteration. So much of the work seemed to be wasted.

Mavis laughed. "You haven't faced enough dead ends then."

Frank raised an eyebrow. "You're talking to a private investigator. I run into more dead ends than correct paths."

"Ever lose a criminal because of one?" asked Mavis.

"A few times," Frank admitted.

"Then you should appreciate iterative deepening," said Mavis. "When I first saw it in action, I was annoyed by the restarts too. But it's saved my life more than once."

"Restarting a search over and over saved your life?" asked Frank.

"Limiting how far I could explore along the wrong path saved my life," corrected Mavis.

"When did iterative deepening save your life?" asked Frank, unable to keep the skepticism from his voice.

Mavis stared out over the ocean. "Well . . . the first time was when I was just a kid. I was an apprentice on a cargo vessel called the *Void Star*. It was an amazing ship; it could carry anything. Anyway, we were lost in the middle of the Razor Ridges—a dense series of volcanic peaks that effectively form a giant maze—and we were running out of important provisions."

"Water?" asked Frank.

"No," answered Mavis. "We had at least two weeks' worth of food and water. We were low on coffee, and that was bad news for the ship's officers. After a single day without coffee, the first mate would get twitchy and sing depressing sea shanties."

"That doesn't sound too bad."

"Without coffee, the man's singing attracted every vicious bird in an eight-mile radius."

Frank winced at the thought.

"Anyway," continued Mavis, "coffee was vital for the ship. The captain estimated we had less than two days to find an island with a supply station. She knew there had to be one close by, but didn't know exactly where. You see, we'd lost the map during an impromptu paper airplane contest. And with the dense fog throughout the ridges, we wouldn't see the station until we were right on top of it."

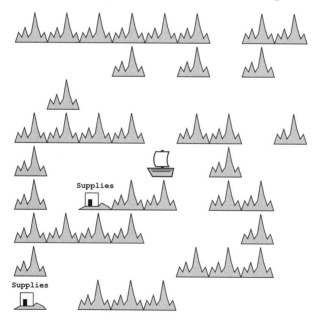

"We started off searching for an island with coffee. I was still green in those days and hadn't heard of iterative deepening, so I boldly suggested a depth-first search. The captain just laughed and told me she'd never trust a depth-first search in the Razor Ridges— too many long dead ends.

"Well. She gridded off the sea into one-mile-square chunks. One mile was about as far as you could see through the fog, so we would need to be in the same grid square as the supply station to see it. Then we set about exploring with iterative deepening. We used a depth-first search, but limited it to a single one-cell step. We used a classic north, east, south, west ordering, backtracking to the starting location each time. We didn't find anything in this first step, but at least we were efficient about it. Within a few hours, we had eliminated all neighboring grid squares.

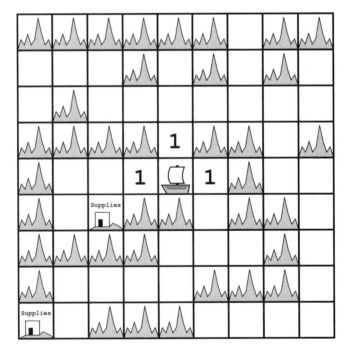

Mavis shook her head. "No sign of the supply station at all. So we started over, doing another depth-first search from the original starting point. This time we explored two steps out and covered a lot more area. We ended up reexploring the neighboring squares in the process. Still no sign of a supply station, but we were able to eliminate all squares within two steps pretty quickly."

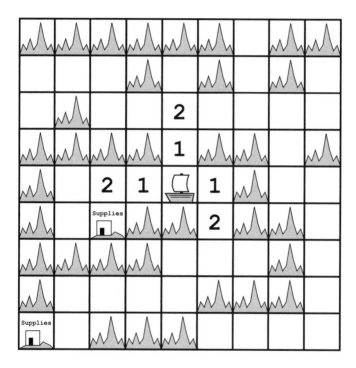

"Why not just use breadth-first search?" asked Frank. "That's what you were effectively doing anyway. Your search explored outward, farther and farther from the starting point."

Mavis nodded. "Breadth-first search and iterative deepening have a lot in common. But you're forgetting one key point. *We had lost our map.* It's really difficult to track your unexplored states in breadth-first search when you don't have a map. How do you remember your frontier? Iterative deepening allowed us to explore outward without having to explicitly remember all the unexplored states. We just followed a depth-limited path."

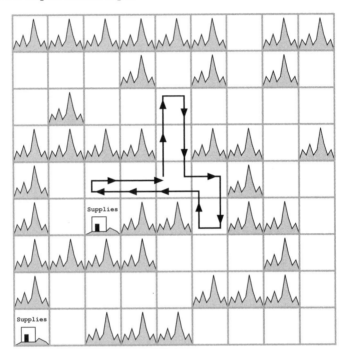

"I guess so," Frank agreed.

"Anyway, we were starting to run low on coffee at that point," Mavis continued. "A group of volunteers, including the captain herself, switched to decaf. But we all knew that would only buy us a little time. We pushed on. We restarted the depth-first search again, this time allowing ourselves to venture out farther."

"Did you find it with a search of length three?" asked Frank.

"Luckily, we did," replied Mavis. "On that iteration we checked everything one, two, and three steps away. By that time, the quartermaster, who had absolutely no use for decaf, had resorted to reusing the same grounds for a 10th time, but the first mate was already singing 'Sea Slugs on Deck.' Fortunately, that was one of his more upbeat tunes."

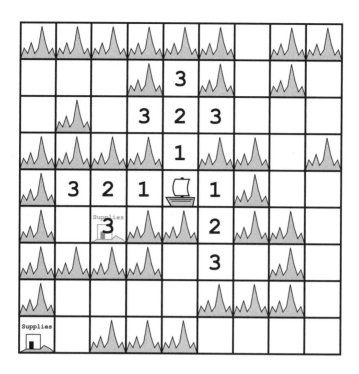

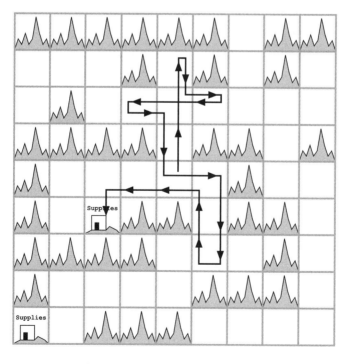

Frank thought about it for a moment. "What if you had skipped the repeated work? What if you had just used depth-first search?"

"We would have gone down a long dead end and run out of coffee," she replied. "Didn't I start by telling you it saved my life?"

"Fair enough. But that's a matter of luck. The nearest supply station could have been down a depth-first search of length five."

"Ha! You know better than that, Frank. You can always find lucky or unlucky problems. Iterative deepening can help you hedge against really unlucky cases. It bounds how far you away you can go on any iteration."

"Other algorithms do that too," he countered.

Mavis scowled. "I didn't say iterative deepening was the *only* algorithm that could have saved us. I said it was the one we used. And I have used it ever since.

"Once I even used it to track down an angry shoal of squid before they inked the capital's harbor. Oh, it would have been a grand mess. Some days I wonder if I should have just let them do it. The king's reaction would have been priceless."

Frank thought for a long while, wondering if iterative deepening could have saved him time here. By cutting off the search sooner, he could have backtracked and followed up on the threads or the mysterious league. But then he wouldn't have been following the highest-priority lead.

He shook his head. "I'll stick with my usual searches," he said finally.

Mavis nodded solemnly and looked out over the ocean. "Fair enough. But be careful, Frank. You don't have much time and long dead ends can be costly. With any algorithm, you should at least think about how to protect yourself from running into the worst-case problems."

POLICE ALGORITHMS 101:
ITERATIVE DEEPENING
Excerpt from Professor Drecker's Lecture

Iterative deepening is a modification of depth-first search that repeatedly performs limited depth-first searches. During iteration (or round) k of iterative deepening, the algorithm performs a depth-limited search with *max-depth* $= k$.

Consider again the example of searching for a suspect starting from city A.

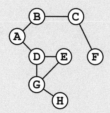

We start with a depth-first search but cut it off after the first node, A. This corresponds to limiting ourselves to searching just the scene of the crime.

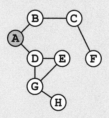

The next iteration restarts the depth-first search but allows it to explore one city away. We cover the close cities, visiting A, B, and D.

continued

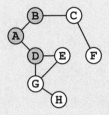

As the search progresses, we have to go farther and farther from the scene of the crime. We end up searching the nearby cities multiple times on different iterations of our search. In fact, we search A four times and B three times.

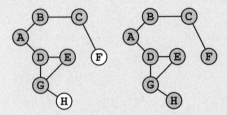

While the repeated work increases computational cost, iterative deepening has advantages. It combines the lower memory requirements of depth-first search with the abilities of breadth-first search to find short paths and avoid getting stuck on some worst-case problems.

— 16 —
Inverted Indexes: The Search Narrows

The gentle tinkle of a bell announced Frank's arrival at Cloaks and More in the center of the capital the next morning. Nearly every square inch of the small shop was packed tight with racks of cloaks. Frank forced his way through a narrow gap between racks toward the counter in the back.

A small balding man peered up through thick glasses. "Welcome to Cloaks and More. I am Gilbert Cloaksworth. How can I help you today?"

He looked Frank up and down. His eyes flicked repeatedly to Frank's well-worn trench cloak, and when he noticed a patch near the shoulder, the shop owner shuddered.

"I see you are in the market for a new cloak," he ventured with the fake cheeriness perfected by snobby shopkeepers the world over. "You have come to the right place. We've just received a wonderful shipment of forest green traveling cloaks."

"I'm looking for information," said Frank. He pulled out the threads from the ArrayCart and held them out to the man. "I need to know what cloak these came from."

Mr. Cloaksworth didn't move. "Not a new cloak?"

"Just information."

"A pity," said Cloaksworth coldly. "But I guess you still came to the right place. I am the city's foremost expert in cloaks." The shop owner took the threads and peered at them for a moment. Then he pulled a large magnifying glass from under the counter and examined them at length.

"Black and orange with a cross-weave stitch," Cloaksworth muttered. "Reasonable quality. Not up to my standards, of course, but reasonable."

"Can you tell me anything else?" prompted Frank. "Something useful perhaps?"

The shop owner scowled, but continued studying the threads. "A trace of charring," he said finally.

"It was in a fire?" Frank asked.

"No. It's too patterned for that. I've only seen this type of charring a few times in my life. Always on wizards' cloaks. This cloak had a spell placed on it."

"Do you know what type?" asked Frank.

Cloaksworth shook his head. "You should ask a wizard. I am the region's foremost expert in cloaks, not spells."

"How about the coloring?" asked Frank. "I haven't seen many cloaks with those colors. Can you tell me anything about where it might be from?"

Cloaksworth smiled. "Of course I can. I am the kingdom's foremost expert in cloaks."

He turned and pulled a gigantic book from a shelf and dropped it on the counter with a loud thud. He flipped to the back.

"What are you doing?" asked Frank.

"Looking up these colors in *The Registry of Cloaks and Heraldry, Volume 5*," responded the shop owner. "You wanted to know where they came from, didn't you?"

"But why are you reading the back of the book?" said Frank. "Shouldn't you be starting at the table of contents?"

Cloaksworth finally gave a genuine smile. "There have been wonderful advances in heraldry tracking the past few years!" he exclaimed. "Traditionally, we did exactly what you suggested: scanned the table of contents for the subject of interest and then flipped to the correct page—using binary search, of course.

"And it is true that the table of contents provides an index into books' subjects. But the table of contents is organized all wrong for this type of search. It lists topics by the order in which they occur. That's a fine ordering if you want to know what comes next, but not if you are looking for a very particular subject. The kingdom now has over 10,000 cloak patterns! It can take a long time just to search the table of contents.

"So Amanda Cloakington, the author *The Registry of Cloaks and Heraldry* and a personal hero of mine, developed the inverted index. She tracked important terms, such as cloak colors, and indexed them in back of the book—almost like a second table of contents."

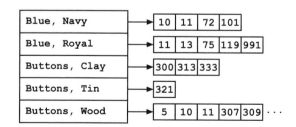

"How does that help?" asked Frank. "She's just repeating the information that's in the table of contents."

"Yes. She repeated information, but she used a different order. She organized the index at the back in order of the terms. Then for each term, she listed the pages where it occurred."

Frank stared at him, waiting. But the owner seemed to have finished. "So?" Frank prompted.

"You only need to look up the term you want, and the index directs you to the corresponding pages!" he exclaimed. "No more muddling through the table of contents. Your search becomes a lookup."

"But you still need to search the index to find the correct term, right?" asked Frank.

"Well, yes. But since the index is sorted alphabetically by the terms, you can just use binary search."

"What if the item appears on a lot of pages?"

"You need to check them all," Cloaksworth conceded.

"What if you are looking for a few terms?" asked Frank. "Like three colors of thread?"

"Ah! Now that's where it gets interesting," said Cloaksworth. "You just need to check the pages they have in common. You can find those by *intersecting* the sets of page numbers. That means going through the lists and finding the elements that occur in *every* list. If you have enough terms, you can usually narrow down the pages they're on to just one or two.

"The other day I had to look up a navy blue and royal blue cloak with wooden buttons. I can tell you that there aren't many of those in the world. In fact, just one group uses that combination—the Association of Amateur Weather Forecasters. Until last year, they had been using navy blue and dark turquoise, but they were forced to change. The Association of Semiprofessional Weather Forecasters claimed, rightfully, that the colors were too similar to their own navy blue and light turquoise."

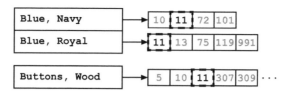

Frank thought about it for a moment and nodded. "Interesting idea," he allowed. He could immediately see how such inverted indexes could be applied to other information sources. Police records were always sorted by date. Using this new technique, you could also index them by the type of crime or the location. These indexes could make research orders of magnitude more efficient.

"I wonder if it'll catch on for other books," Frank mused.

"Unlikely," the shop owner scoffed. "Few topics in this world are complicated enough to require an index. Not every topic is as rich as cloakology."

As he spoke, the shop owner searched through the index and proceeded to flip rapidly through the book. "Police cloak," he said at last. "The departments of Bool and Functionia use those colors. So do a few of the capital police force's departments. Accounting, Payroll, Records, and Advisory Signage, I believe. All different designs, of course. I expect the cloak is a new issue, given the state of the threads. Police officers have a tendency to wear out cloaks quickly, especially in the Department of Advisory Signage."

"A new police cloak?" Frank confirmed.

"Most likely," said Cloaksworth. "I doubt it is a custom design. Those colors were popular 20 years ago, but fell out of favor with the rise of pastels. It's a shame, really—there were some beautiful cloaks back in those days. I once made a riding cloak with double fastenings and—"

Frank interrupted him, "Anything else you can tell me about the threads?"

The shop owner looked at him. "Aside from the fact that they are probably from a new police cloak from one of four departments and it was enchanted with a magic spell?"

Frank waited.

"Uh . . . no," said Cloaksworth finally. "That's everything."

Frank nodded. "Thanks," he said. He picked up the threads and turned to leave. He heard a soft gasp as he opened the door and knew the shop owner had seen the ragged edge at the bottom of his trench cloak.

POLICE ALGORITHMS 101: INVERTED INDEXES
Excerpt from Professor Drecker's Lecture

An inverted index is a computational data structure similar to the index of a book. It provides a mapping from target values to the location in the data where those values occur. Inverted indexes are especially useful when a given value occurs, or might occur, repeatedly throughout the data.

Consider an example from our lecture on binary search— checking an accounting ledger for transactions with a particular merchant. The ledgers are sorted by increasing transaction number, indicating the order in which the transactions were recorded.

101	August 16	Zed's Coffee	8.00
102	August 15	Bob's Pizza	20.00
103	August 15	Wands and More	150.00
104	August 15	Spell Shoppe	100.00
105	August 16	Zed's Coffee	8.00
106	August 16	Spell Shoppe	50.00
107	August 17	Zed's Coffee	8.00
108	August 17	Hospital	250.00

While this ordering allows us to efficiently find information for a given transaction ID, it doesn't help us trace transactions to a particular merchant. One option would be to re-sort the entries by merchant name. However, this requires us to make a copy of the entire ledger, which can be costly.

Instead, we can build an additional data structure: an inverted index, keyed by merchant name. For each merchant, we then store just a list of all the relevant transaction IDs. Since we already know how to efficiently look up any transaction given its ID, we can now get from merchant name to transaction information via an additional lookup in our index.

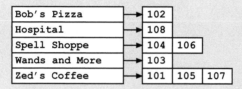

Inverted indexes are a great example of a common trade-off between running time and memory usage. An algorithm can trade an increase in memory usage, in the form of an additional index, for significantly more efficient searches along a new dimension.

A Binary Search Tree Trap

L ess than a block from Cloaks and More, Frank spotted a woman tailing him. Even as irritation flashed through him, he had to admit that she was good. She kept to the other side of the road, always at least 30 feet back. More often than not, she relied on the reflections in the shop windows to watch him. And she wore a perfectly nondescript traveling cloak—a shade of forest green sported by over half the people on the street.

Frank stopped abruptly, dropped to one knee, and pretended to tie his shoe. It was the second oldest technique for identifying a tail, the first being to dash madly in a random direction and see who followed. Although arguably less effective than a mad dash, the fake-shoe-tying routine had the benefit of subtlety and, more importantly, involved no running.

The tail continued on past, stopping about 10 feet ahead to examine a stack of cabbages through a particularly well-polished shop window.

Frank stood and started back in the other direction. After half a block, he crossed to her side of the street, ignoring the angry shouts from a donkey cart driver, and started down a small alley. Once off the main road, he turned around and waited.

The tail almost ran into him as she hurried around the corner.

"Hi," said Frank. "Why are you following me?" He tried for a conversational, nonchalant tone—something he couldn't pull off even under normal circumstances. It was at best a growl, though he did manage to avoid shouting.

Professional spies often devote considerable time to planning how they will react if discovered. They develop a portfolio of complex backstories for a range of scenarios, explaining away everything from following someone to being discovered in the royal palace with a listening device and a fake turtle. They dream of smooth recoveries and effortless lies. However, things rarely go so well in reality, and gasps of surprise are actually quite common. In this case, Frank had even been hoping for a moment of panic to exploit.

True to form, however, the tail remained professional. There was no panic. There was no gasp of surprise. The only indication that anything had gone wrong was the briefest flash of anger in her eyes right before she flung down a smoke bomb and vanished.

Even without the smoke bomb, the spy would have been too fast for Frank. By the time he grabbed for her, he could hear her footsteps pounding down the street. He cursed and plunged through the smoke after her.

Within half a block, Frank had resigned himself to yet another depth-first search. He had chased enough petty thieves through the city to know how it would go. The spy would likely turn off the main road soon, hoping to get out of sight. It wasn't a bad strategy in general, but it wouldn't work here. This part of the city had few side streets, and most of them were dead ends.

As he ran, he visualized the streets as a graph, with the intersections and dead ends as nodes where he would have to make decisions and the roads in between as the graph's edges—paths that got him from one decision point to another.

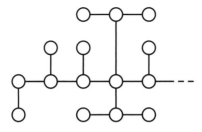

Doing a quick calculation, he figured he had time to explore maybe five or six side streets before he fell too far behind and the trail went cold. Unfortunately, that was just one of the risks of using depth-first search for a chase.

The first two streets proved to be a waste of time. The closest thing he found to criminal activity was a pack of kids covering the wall with graffiti. Using a charred stick, they had written "Team recursion" and "Recursion 4eva." He continued his search.

A few more dead ends later, Frank was contemplating giving up when he spotted a trail of footprints in the mud leading to an open sewer grate. He leaned against the wall and caught his breath. This had to be her escape route.

Frank peered into the dark hole but couldn't see anything. He lowered himself through the sewer grate and dropped onto a wooden platform. He crouched low, making himself as small a target as possible, and scanned the dark room. The platform was bolted to a rough stone wall, overlooking a cavernous room that extended at least 50 feet down. The only light streamed in through the opening above, shining down like a giant spotlight on the distant floor. As he watched, the spy streaked through the oval of light and ran toward the opposite wall. She was well ahead of him now.

Frank surveyed his options. There were other platforms below him, about 20 feet apart and connected by iron ladders. When he noticed the small brass tag embedded in the floor, he swore vigorously. He was standing at the top of a binary search ladder.

Binary search ladders were originally designed by Alena Branche, an eccentric art gallery owner, as a way to organize paintings. They were effectively giant binary search trees—data structures designed to allow efficient searches. The structure is organized like a giant upside-down tree, with a single platform at the top, known technically as the *root node*. Branching down from each platform is a maximum of two ladders, each of which leads to a different *child node*—another platform one level below. The entire structure branches and branches as it descends, offering a variety of paths.

A fanatic about the tiniest details, Alena had originally used this structure to organize paintings by the number of grass blades depicted. She enforced a simple organizational scheme: when standing on any platform, you were guaranteed that all paintings below the left ladder (in the left *subtree*) would contain fewer blades of grass than the current platform's picture. And all paintings below the right ladder (in the right *subtree*) would contain more. By starting at the top, you could even choose your path down so as to find a painting with a particular number of grass blades.

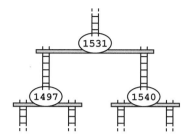

Unfortunately, these kinds of binary search ladders never really caught on in the art world, due to both their excessive size and the need for constant climbing, but they were quickly adopted and adapted by the criminal world. Binary search ladder traps, the dangerous implementation of Alena's creation, had been developed by junior wizard Katia Ladderfell while she was working for the Vinettees. Instead of paintings, Katia placed a single numeric tag on each platform and created a numeric password that would allow safe passage through the tree. When designing a tree and placing the tags, she maintained the binary search tree property—the values in any node's left subtree were always less than at the node itself, and the values in the right subtree were always greater. Only one path through this new weaponized binary search tree was safe, and that was the path that led to the password value at the bottommost node. If you knew the password, you could descend the tree as though performing a search for that value. At each level, you could compare the password's value to the value on the current platform and choose the left or right ladder accordingly. Thus, the Vinettees' thugs were required to memorize only a single password instead of a series of ladder choices. This simplicity was essential given the quality of the organization's help.

If you didn't know the password and chose a wrong ladder, you triggered sometimes deadly and sometimes just emotionally scarring traps. Typical dangers included cursed ladders, poisonous spiders, falling rocks, dart guns, swinging blades, and in some cases magical insults—where intruders would be demoralized by five levels of progressively nasty observations on the state of their appearance, odor, or general intelligence.

The last time Frank had faced one of the Vinettees' binary search ladders, a snitch had given him the password—the number 10. This one number allowed Frank to sneak into the hideout undetected and catch three of the Vinettees by surprise. Only Rebecca had escaped.

If only he knew the password to this trap, he might still have a chance of catching the spy.

A series of ideas flickered through Frank's mind in quick succession. First, why wouldn't the Vinettees reuse passwords? Their thugs tended to be rather dim individuals. Frank doubted they could remember more than a few numbers. Second, there weren't really any evil wizards around anymore, so this binary search ladder trap must have been constructed years ago. After the wizard Exponentious's failed attempt to bring down the kingdom, the lesser evil wizards had either reformed or gone into hiding. In fact, Katia Ladderfell herself had fled town to start a coconut farm. Finally, Frank was extremely high up and his knees were starting to feel weak.

Frank eyed the tag on the root node platform on which he stood: 50. If he was correct and the Vinettees had reused the password, he needed to search down the ladders for 10. Since 10 is less than 50, he needed to go down the left subtree.

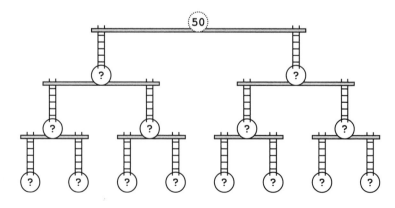

Mumbling a string of preemptive curses, Frank moved toward the left-hand ladder and started down. The journey proved gratifyingly uneventful. No spiders. No swinging blades. Not even a single insult.

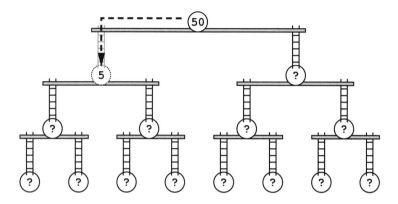

On the next platform, Frank found a tag labeled 5. Since 10 is greater than 5, he knew the path was to the right this time. He jogged to the right-hand ladder, growing in confidence. It often paid to trust in others' incompetence.

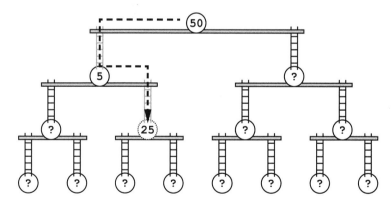

The next platform sat one level, and 20 feet, above the ground. Frank noted that the tag read 25 and immediately went left.

He had descended halfway before he realized something was wrong. He heard a soft screech as the rung above his left foot started to move. He glanced down just in time to see it hit the bar below, crunching his left foot between the rungs. He shouted in surprise. As he watched, the rung slid up and then down again, sending a fresh jolt of pain through his foot. The ladder was literally biting him. He could even feel ridges of metallic teeth start to poke out along each rung.

Making a split-second decision, he jumped clear before the ladder could start chomping at his fingers. He landed awkwardly on his twice-bitten foot, staggering a few steps before easing himself to the floor.

He swivelled around and glared at the tag at the bottom of the ladder. The tag clearly read 10. He had taken the correct path. Then he noticed a small chalk notation on the floor nearby. It read "Do not use. Password changed." Frank promptly resumed his swearing.

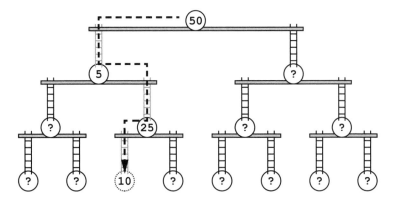

POLICE ALGORITHMS 101:
BINARY SEARCH TREES
Excerpt from Professor Drecker's Lecture

A binary search tree is a data structure that organizes data similarly to how it would be accessed in an ordinary binary search. Each tree node stores a single value and can have up to two child nodes: a left child and a right child. The tree nodes are organized by the values they contain. The values of the data in the left node (and all its children) will be lower than the value of the current node. Similarly, the values of the data in the right node (and all its children) will be greater than the value of the current node.

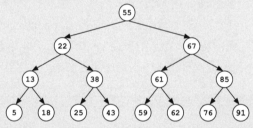

We can efficiently search the binary search tree by walking down from the topmost node—also called the *root node.* At each step, we determine whether to explore the left or right subtree by comparing the value at the current node with the target value. If the target value is less than the current value, the search progresses to the left:

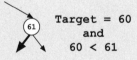

continued

If the target value is greater than the current value, the search progresses to the right:

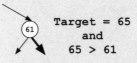

The search ends when either the target value is found or we reach a dead end. In the latter case, we can definitively say that the target value is not in the tree.

We say that the binary search tree is perfectly balanced if every node in the tree has the same number of nodes in its left subtree as in its right subtree. In this case, the depth of the tree grows by one each time we approximately double the number of nodes in the tree.

The computational cost of a search is proportional to the depth of the target value in the tree. The deeper the tree, the more comparisons we have to perform.

— 18 —
Building Binary Search Ladders

Y ou didn't think we would change the password, Mr. Runtime?"
asked a voice behind Frank.

Frank whipped his head around. The spy was strolling toward
him, calm and unhurried. Frank tried to stand, but his left foot
protested with a burst of pain. He settled for scooting around on his
butt until he faced her.

"I didn't think the Vinettees would have the ability to change it,"
Frank admitted. "It's hard to find an evil wizard these days. I hear
their last wizard is selling coconuts now."

"Difficult, yes. So many of the best evil wizards fled or took positions of commercially viable neutrality. However, it is not impossible
to find help. Let's just say the Vinettees were able to make a suitable
arrangement. They have found a wizard who is willing to provide
certain magical assistance in exchange for their services in other
areas."

She waved toward the ladders. "Admittedly, he isn't as talented
as Katia when it comes to binary search tree traps. She was a true
artist. But his work is sufficient."

"Believe it or not, you almost made it down. You were one ladder
off. The password is 26. We obviously didn't want him changing too

many ladders—just enough to trap anyone who tried to reuse an old password. So close."

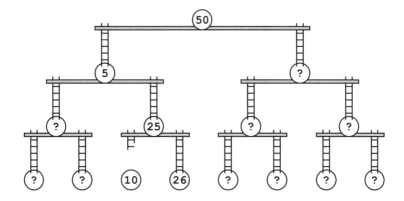

Frank remained silent, but when she didn't continue, he asked, "Who are you?"

"My name is not important. I work for the Vinettees."

"A spy?"

She shrugged. "I collect information. Call it what you want."

"What do you want with me?"

"We want you out of the way, obviously."

Frank considered the implications. It would take more than a bitten foot to sideline him, and the spy had to know this. Which meant that she planned to either kill him or keep him captive. While neither option appealed to Frank, he always preferred the one that didn't involved getting killed.

As though reading his thoughts, the spy responded, "I had hoped the binary search ladder trap would do the job, but no. Not yet, at least." She walked over to another ladder just past 26 and struck a rung with the palm of her hand. A dull

gonging sound filled the room. Then she struck again twice more. *Gong. Gong.*

"Goodbye, Mr. Runtime," she said. And, without so much as a backward glance, she strode from the room.

Confused, Frank watched her go. Then movement out of the corner of his eye caught his attention. As he watched, three rungs detached themselves and dropped to the floor. After a moment, they started wriggling toward him, hissing quietly. Snake rungs.

Frank moved quickly. The snake rungs were dangerous but slow. If he could make it to ladder 26, he still had a chance. He crawled on his hands and knees, not trusting his foot yet. He used the ladder to pull himself to his feet and leaned heavily against the metal. There was no doubt about it, this climb was going to hurt.

The snake rungs were just a few feet away now.

With a groan of annoyance, Frank reached up and started to climb the ladder. It was more of a hop than a climb; he had to jump off his good foot and pull himself to the next rung. His left foot throbbed with each movement.

Frank hauled himself up to the top and collapsed onto platform 25, lying back to catch his breath and curse binary search ladders. To think that he had once thought these structures beautiful, elegant even. He had been to several of Alena's exhibits during his police academy days and had even attended the world's one and only instance of binary search tree performance art.

The exhibit had been called *Raise the Pears.* Alena had contracted three wizards to magically raise a binary search ladder in real time, organizing a collection of paintings by the number of pears they depicted. Pear-centric still life had been a craze that year, a phenomenon later blamed on the poor quality of the apple crop. While not as embarrassing as the following year's obsession with toast sculptures, the pear craze is still only ever discussed in art history classes, and even there only in hushed tones, with the appropriate expression of disgust.

Seven assistants, each carrying a crude painting containing pears, had paraded into the gallery. They stood in sorted order from 1 to 23 pears, the paintings held in front of their faces to hide their shame at the absurd spectacle.

The first wizard stepped forward. He counted out the pictures, finding the middle element. The painting depicted eight pears and a cup of milk on a wooden table.

"Tree root ascend," the wizard shouted. Immediately the line of paintings split into three groups. On the left were the paintings with fewer than eight pears. On the right were the paintings with more than eight pears. And floating above them was the new root of the binary search tree. He had made the first branch.

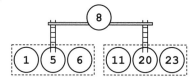

After that, the other two wizards recursively divided the paintings on each side, first left and then right. The process was always the same. The wizard selected the middle element and partitioned the paintings based on that element. As they worked, the tree rose into the air and branched out below the root node.

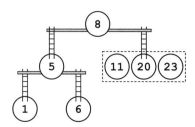

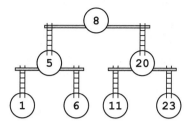

At the time, the demonstration had seemed amazing. Now, sitting on the weaponized form of the data structure, Frank found the whole concept rather idiotic. He wondered how he could have ever thought the recursive division of paintings was beautiful.

The sound of hissing brought Frank back to the moment. The end of a snake rung poked up onto the platform and swiveled around, searching for Frank. Given that it was little more than an animated piece of metal, Frank wasn't exactly sure how the snake rung searched. It didn't have any eyes, nose, or mouth. Maybe it sensed vibrations.

He considered kicking the snake rung down, but decided against it. Snake rungs were inexplicably poisonous, considering their lack of a mouth.

Instead, Frank decided to continue his retreat. He scooted over to the upward ladder and hoisted himself into a standing position. The pain in his ankle had subsided enough to make the next climb more of a traditional ladder experience and less a frantic hopping motion.

Frank continued directly up the next level, returning to the top root-node platform with the little brass tag reading 50.

He paused to mutter yet another curse against binary search ladders. They were, as he saw it now, quite stupid contraptions. Despite not having any actual reasoning behind it, Frank felt confident in his assessment. With a satisfied nod, he pulled himself back onto the street and away from the snake rungs.

POLICE ALGORITHMS **101**:
BINARY SEARCH TREES
Excerpt from Professor Drecker's Lecture

You can create binary search trees from a sorted array by recursively dividing the elements into smaller subsets. At each level, the middle value is chosen as the node at that level. If there is an even number of elements, you can use either of the two middle elements.

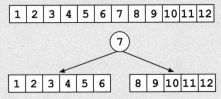

Once the root node has been created, both the left and right subsets will then independently split in the same way. Conceptually, we split the sorted array into left and right arrays and apply the same algorithm on each of those arrays.

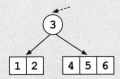

Note that during construction, it is not actually necessary to split or copy the array. The algorithm can use a single array by simply tracking the indexes of the lowest and highest value in the current branch.

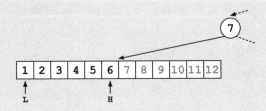

Binary Search Trees for Suspects

Frank limped back into his office to find Socks waiting. The young wizard sat in Frank's chair, spinning idly. Frank glared until Socks realized his mistake. He mumbled an apology and jumped out of the chair.

"What did you find?" Frank asked.

Socks shrugged. "Nothing useful."

"Nothing?" Frank prompted.

"None of the wizards had heard of any new leagues," Socks added quickly. "The last wizarding league formed was the League of Magical Confectioners. They formed last year in response to the influx of subpar mints. Do you remember those grainy tablets restaurants served? They tasted like mint for the first few minutes but left an aftertaste of pine needles for the next six hours. It was like they were meant to be a prank. The League of Magical Confectioners fixed the mint situation, and then branched out into chocolates and toffees. The league now has six candy shops and four carts—"

"Nothing else?" Frank interrupted.

Socks shook his head. "I also asked about clubs and associations," he offered. "The only new one was the Babbageville Wizards

Bowling Association, and they lasted less than a month. Apparently there just aren't that many wizards in Babbageville who like to bowl."

Frank sighed. He hadn't expected much from Socks's investigation, but the complete lack of news still managed to disappoint him.

"How about you?" Socks asked.

"Yeah," replied Frank. "I got a new lead."

"Really? What is it?"

Before Frank could answer, Officer Notation banged noisily into the office carrying an absurdly large stack of books. She made it to Frank's desk and dropped the stack. The desk sagged under the weight.

"All the transfer and assignment ledgers for the past year," she panted. "Now can you tell me why I dragged these here?"

"We need to find a transfer," said Frank.

"I figured that," said Notation. "But if you'd told me which transfer, I could have just looked it up there."

"I don't know which transfer," explained Frank. It was half true. Even if he had known, he would have still asked Notation to bring up all the records. He needed to be there during the search. He needed to make sure no one was missed.

"Okay," said Notation. "What are we looking for?"

"We'll start with any suspicious transfer between 50 and 70 days ago," said Frank. Those were the approximate dates of the pages that had been torn from the ledger in the prison. "It's a range search. We want to find all the transfers in a range of dates."

Notation groaned. "These requests are sorted by the original location of the requesting officer and then by officer name. They aren't indexed by the date of the request. We'll have to go through every request. It'll take hours."

"No, it won't," Frank assured her. "Because we're going to use magic."

Socks looked up in surprise. "Magic?" he asked. "I don't know any range search spells."

"You know binary search trees," responded Frank.

"I'm an expert on binary search trees," agreed Socks, "but I don't see how that helps."

"We can build a binary search tree of transfer requests, with each node's value equal to how long ago the transfer occurred. Then we can do a range search on the tree."

"Range search on the tree?" asked Socks.

"Why bother with a tree?" asked Notation. "If we're just doing one search, it'll take longer to build the tree than to scan through the data."

Frank shrugged. "My guess is that we'll ultimately want to do more than one search. If Socks builds the tree with magic, we can search it a bunch of times."

"But I don't know how to do a range search," Socks protested.

"Build the tree and I'll show you."

"Okay," said Socks. "This'll take a little while; I'm only used to working with buttons. Real, physical buttons. I've never had to organize facts before. Facts seem like they'll be squishy. I'll need to modify the spell."

As Socks hunched over Frank's desk and scrawled out a modified spell on a piece of parchment, Notation confronted Frank. "What's going on?" she asked.

"Nothing," Frank said.

"Oh, come off it," Notation snapped. "Ever since the prison, you've been holding something back. Why are we looking at transfer requests? How come you never mentioned them before? What did you find?"

"As I said, it's a hunch."

"I don't buy it. You aren't telling me something."

Frank didn't answer.

"Got it," called Socks. "I think so, at least. We'll see in a minute."

Socks turned to the stack of ledgers and began muttering an incantation. He waved his arms dramatically but entirely unnecessarily over the paper. With a flash, a large binary search tree appeared in the air with each node in the tree representing the number of days since that transfer date. The nodes hung in the air, connected by electric blue lines.

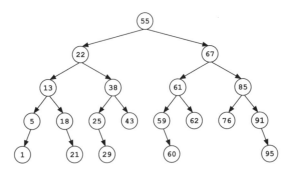

"Now we range search," said Frank.

"I told you, I don't—" started Socks, but Frank waved him off.

"We'll use a modified depth-first search," Frank explained. "Start at the top node, the root node, and explore down the tree."

"Explore how?" asked Socks.

"At each node, you follow three steps. First, you check if the node itself falls into the range. If it does, like 55 days here, then we'll save it to our list of results. Otherwise, we ignore it."

"Hold on a second," said Socks. "I'll make the nodes in our list glow a different color. What about dark green?"

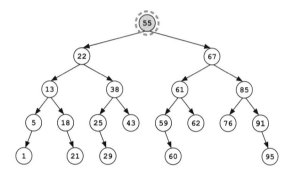

"Sure. Whatever," Frank replied. "After we check the current node, we check whether we need to explore either child node. We recursively explore the left and right subtrees if, and only if, they could have nodes in the correct range."

"Recursively explore?" asked Socks.

Frank waited for Notation to jump in with one of her formal definitions, but she remained stubbornly silent. He sighed and explained, "*Recursively* just means we apply the same algorithm to subproblems. In this case, we apply the same search to each of the child nodes. We treat them the same way we do the root node.

"Just check whether we need to explore the children, and, if so, apply the same steps. We'll use a simple test and compare the *current* node's value with our range. If the current node's value is *less* than the *lower* end of the range, we know everything in the left subtree would fall below our range and we can skip that subtree. Alternatively, if the current node's value is *greater* than the *lower* end of our range, we will need to continue our search on the left child.

"The same logic applies to the right subtree. If the current node's value is *greater* than the *higher* end of our range, we can skip the right subtree. Otherwise, we repeat our search on the right child.

"In this case, our range is 50 to 70, and as the left child can have values up to 55, nodes in that subtree could fall within our range, so we need to explore the left child. The right child can have values above 55, which also overlaps our range, so we need to explore that as well. Start with the left child.

"Now we have 22 days," continued Frank. "We don't put it on our list. And because everything in the left subtree has to be less than 22, we don't need to explore down that path either."

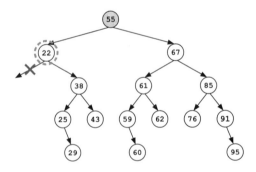

"We call this *pruning* the exploration," added Notation. "Because it's like cutting off the branch of a tree."

When Frank looked over, she scowled as she remembered she wasn't talking to him and fell silent.

"So we only explore the right child," said Frank.

"Recursively!" added Socks with all too much glee.

"Yes, recursively," agreed Frank dryly. "Now we get 38. Again, it doesn't go on the list, and we can skip the left branch."

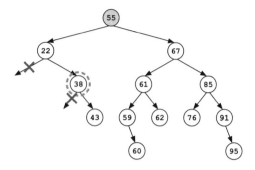

"But we need to recursively explore the right branch," said Socks, who was thoroughly enjoying the new algorithm.

Frank nodded.

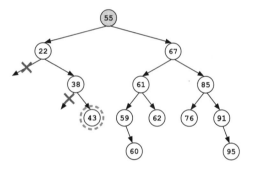

The next node had no children. It was a dead end.

"Now what?" asked Socks.

"Same thing as in a depth-first search," said Frank. "We backtrack and take unexplored paths until we've searched the whole tree. In this case, we've already pruned a lot of paths, so we need to backtrack to the root."

The search progressed down the root's right subtree. New matches were added to the result list, incompatible paths were pruned, and compatible paths were explored recursively.

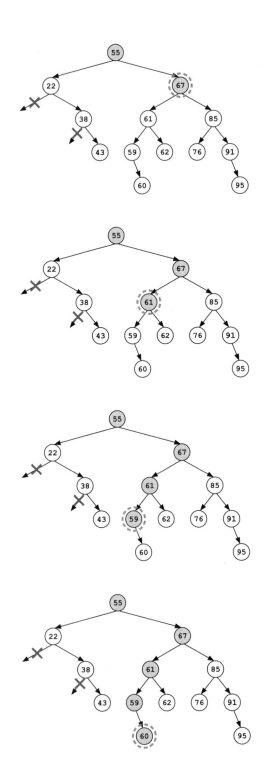

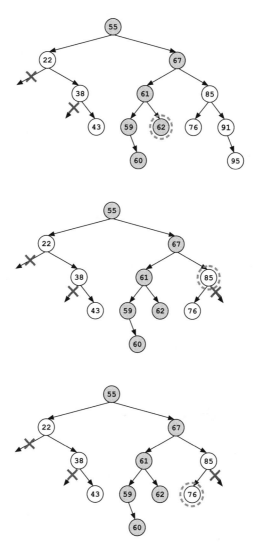

By the end, they had identified a handful of transfers that fell within the target range. Frank studied the list intently, looking for anything suspicious.

"Nothing," he growled in disbelief. "There's nothing here."

POLICE ALGORITHMS 101:
BINARY SEARCH TREES
Excerpt from Professor Drecker's Lecture

The range search algorithm on a binary search tree is similar to the search for a single value. The algorithm starts at the top node and recursively explores down the tree. At each node, it makes decisions based on three questions:

1. **Should this node be added to the results?** The current value should be added to the results if, and only if, it falls within the range.

2. **Should the left subtree be explored?** The algorithm should recursively explore the left subtree if there is a left child and the value of the current node is *greater than* the smallest value in the range. In that case, there *could* be a node in the left subtree that falls within the range.

3. **Should the right subtree be explored?** The algorithm should recursively explore the right subtree if there is a right child and the value of the current node is *less than* the largest value in the range. In that case, there *could* be a node in the right subtree that falls within the range.

The advantage of using a binary search tree for range search is that you may be able to save computation by pruning out large amounts of the search space.

Consider the following binary tree:

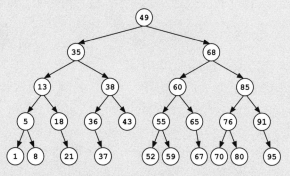

If you are searching for all values within the range [8, 20], you need to visit and evaluate only 7 of the 25 nodes (visited nodes are shaded):

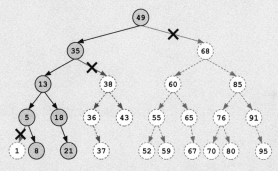

Similarly, if you are searching within the range [70, 80], you need to visit and evaluate only 6 of the 25 nodes:

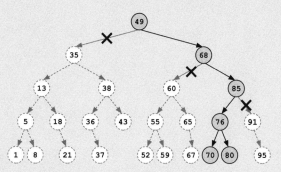

continued

It's important to note that visiting a node doesn't necessarily mean that it will appear in the result list. Both of the example searches still have to visit nodes that fall outside the range, because those nodes' subtrees could contain values within the range.

As with a search for a single value, using a binary search tree for range search is efficient only if you're conducting multiple searches. Constructing a binary search tree is more expensive than doing a linear scan through the data. However, the cost of building a tree can be spread out over many searches to make the average cost per search lower.

Adding Suspects to the Search Tree

Frank studied the list of transfers for a few more minutes but failed to see anything suspicious. None of the recent transfer destinations were even remotely close to the capital, where most of the thefts had occurred. The nearest transfer had been to the city of Easterville—50 miles away—and the "Reason for Transfer" listed by the young officer's captain had been "a persistent smell of feet."

"This is everyone?" Frank asked, turning to Notation.

"Yes," said Notation defensively. "This is every officer who transferred between stations in the last year."

Frank frowned. The definition sounded wrong to him. It sounded incomplete. "What about initial transfers?" asked Frank.

"From the academy?" asked Notation.

"Yes," said Frank. "What about transfers from the academy?"

"Well," said Notation. "Those would be probationary initial transfers. They would be recorded in different ledgers."

Frank nodded slowly. His mind raced.

"I can get—" Notation started.

"No need," Frank interrupted. "I promised the captain an update by this afternoon. I can pick up the ledgers then."

"You're going to see the captain?" asked Notation, surprised.

"Updating your clients is part of the life of a private eye," said Frank.

"You can also tell the captain about Gretchen's theory," added Socks.

"What theory?" asked Notation, her eyes darting between Frank and Socks.

"Frank didn't tell you?" asked Socks.

"No," said Notation, through clenched teeth, "he did not." Her hands were balled into fists at her side, but her face clearly said that she would very much prefer to use one of them to punch Frank in the nose.

"My mentor Gretchen thinks there will be an attack on the castle tomorrow night," said Socks.

"She does?" asked Notation. Then, turning to Frank, she added, "That seems like a useful piece of information. Why didn't you tell me?"

"It's just speculation," replied Frank with a shrug, but he avoided her eye.

"I should come with you to see the captain," said Notation.

Frank balked. He hadn't expected that. People usually dreaded updating Captain Donovan unless they could open the conversation with "Great news!" or "You'll never guess what we found." Going into his office with an update consisting of equal parts dead ends, unexplored leads, and life-threatening situations invited a loud and colorful lecture. Frank wouldn't even be considering it if he didn't need information himself.

"I need you to follow up on something else," said Frank after only a brief pause. "Parallelized search, remember?" He reached into his pocket and felt around but found only his notepad, a few food wrappers, and an old empty snail shell. The shell was a souvenir from his last case, a nasty affair involving a percussion band and numerous noise complaints. He pulled it from his pocket.

"See if you can find out anything about this," he said.

"A shell?" Notation asked. "What does it have to do with the case?"

"I don't know," Frank hedged. "But Glass Box Billy might."

Reluctantly, Notation took the shell and studied it. As she turned it over in her hands, she muttered, "Why does it have to be Billy? He's always impossible to find."

Frank turned to Socks, who was staring at the shell with a profoundly confused expression. "Can you maintain the binary search tree on our way to the station?"

"Uh, sure," said Socks. "But it would be easier to just build a new one."

Frank shook his head. "We'd need all these ledgers for that, and I don't feel like lugging them halfway across the city. They look heavy."

At that, Notation interrupted her investigation of the shell to shoot him another nasty look.

Fifty-seven minutes later, Frank and Socks stood outside the police records office. The trip usually took less than 20 minutes, but they were slowed significantly by the large glowing binary search tree floating in front of Socks. Not only did it block his vision, causing him to trip over numerous ruts, but it was also the cause of much rubbernecking and endless questions from curious pedestrians, until Frank resorted to yelling "Out of the way! Dangerously unstable magic here," as they walked. The warning worked quite well.

"Don't you need to speak with the captain?" asked Socks.

"First we find our transfer," said Frank. He never liked going into a meeting with a client empty-handed.

Every class at the police academy produced around 20 new officers, each of whom transferred to a station somewhere in the kingdom. As a result, the Ledger of Initial Assignments for the last 10 classes weighed at least 10 pounds. As with the other transfer ledgers, it was sorted by name rather than date.

"It looks like we have a couple hundred transfers to add to the tree," Frank said as he found an empty desk in the paperwork common room. Due to the standard combination of security needs and high volumes of paperwork, no one was allowed to work in the records vault itself. Instead, all police stations included one or more workrooms immediately adjacent to the record room, containing nothing more than long wooden tables and individual study carrels.

"We can't just add nodes!" Socks exclaimed.

"Of course we can," said Frank. "Adding to a binary search tree is easy. Start at the top, search downward as though you're looking for the element and, when you hit a dead end, add the new entry below that node.

"Take this first transfer, 57 days ago. We start at the top. Because 57 is larger than the root node's value of 55, we go to the right. Then we go left, because 57 is less than 67. Then we go left again, because 57 is less than 61. Finally, comparing 57 to 59, we ought to go down to the left node again, but we can't because there is no left child. So we add the new node as the left child of 59."

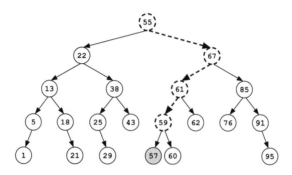

Socks looked horrified.

"Here," said Frank. "I'll show you again. This transfer was 89 days ago. We go right, then right, then right again. And we add it as the left child of 91, because 89 is less than 91."

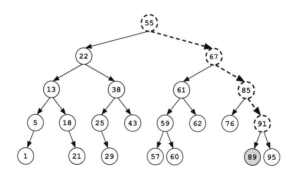

"That's not what I mean," insisted Socks. "What if the tree becomes unbalanced?"

"It could happen," admitted Frank. "When you're adding elements to a binary search tree, the resulting tree might be unbalanced. Our search algorithm will still work, though."

"But searches could be inefficient on an unbalanced tree," protested Socks.

"That's true," admitted Frank.

Adding nodes to a tree could cancel out one of the major advantages of a balanced binary search tree: that it makes many algorithms efficient. Each time you approximately double the number of nodes in a balanced binary search tree, you only need to add a single level. This means that for a simple search, such as looking up an element, you can double the amount of data while adding only one more step to your search. However, Socks was correct: this efficiency applies only if the tree is balanced. In the worst case, the tree forms a long line that you're forced to search along. And when you're adding arbitrary values, there are no guarantees that the tree will remain balanced.

"We'll have to risk it," Frank declared finally.

"But—"

"If our search isn't as efficient as it could be, I'm willing to live with that. It's a small price to pay for not having to carry those other books with us to build the tree from scratch. They looked heavy."

POLICE ALGORITHMS 101:
BINARY SEARCH TREES
Excerpt from Professor Drecker's Lecture

Adding nodes to a binary search tree is similar to searching for a target value. We start at the root of the tree and progress downward as though searching for the value to insert. We progress to the left or right depending on whether the new value we're inserting is smaller or larger than the value at the current node. The descent ends when we reach a dead end: a node without a child in the correct direction. At this point, we can create a new node and make it the (left or right) child.

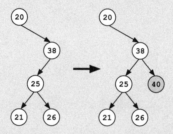

The cost of inserting a single element scales linearly with the depth of the tree. However, we have no guarantees that the tree will remain balanced as new nodes are inserted. In fact, it is easy for a tree to become unbalanced, with deep branches, depending on the order of insertions. For example, if we insert numbers in sorted order, all the additions can go down a single branch.

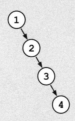

The Binary Search Tree Property

W ait," Frank said. "That's wrong."

Socks, who had just finished inserting a node, looked up in surprise. "What?"

"The node you just inserted," said Frank. "It's in the wrong place."

Socks peered at the tree. "But 63 is larger than 60, so it goes in the right-hand subtree."

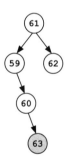

"But it's greater than its great-grandparent 61, so it should have gone to that node's right subtree. You have it down the left subtree. One of the key properties of a binary search tree is that *all* nodes in the left subtree are less than the current node, and *all* nodes in the right subtree are larger."

"I know that," said Socks quietly.

"Then why is it in the left subtree?" Frank asked.

"I made a mistake," said Socks.

"How did you miss that 63 is larger than 61?" Frank asked.

"I . . . I started at 60," Socks admitted.

"What?"

"Well, I had recently inserted node 60 . . . and 63 is close to 60 . . . so I just started at 60 and inserted it below that."

"You didn't start at the root?" Frank snapped.

"I figured this would be faster," said Socks. "I got to skip down most of the tree."

"You ended up putting it in the wrong place. How many other shortcuts have you taken?"

"A few," admitted Socks.

Frank groaned, then, for good measure, muttered a long string of curses. Socks stared at the ground and wisely said nothing.

After he had finally calmed down, Frank took a few deep breaths and surveyed the tree.

"We'll have to do an exhaustive search," he said through gritted teeth. "If the tree doesn't maintain the binary search tree property, we can't safely do any pruning. We'll have to check each node."

"Hey," said Socks suddenly. "We had to check each node to put it in the tree. Why didn't we just do an exhaustive search then?"

"Amortized cost," Frank said. "I was hoping to use the tree for a bunch of searches in the future. I doubt 50 days to 70 days will be the only range we search. As we get more evidence, we might do different range searches. Maybe we would even need to do a few exact searches. The cost of building the tree would be averaged out over many searches, and the overall effort would be lower—possibly much lower. Amortized cost considers the total cost for a bunch of searches and thus spreads the cost of building the tree over many searches."

"Oh," said Socks. "Like my magic button trees."

Frank fought the urge to shake the young wizard and yell, "Of course like the button tree! They're both binary search trees. They both benefit from a one-time construction cost by making many subsequent searches faster." Instead, he settled for a snarky "Of course."

"Great idea," said Socks. "We can save lots of time in the future."

"Could have saved," Frank corrected him.

"Oh," said Socks. "Right. I broke the tree, didn't I?"

POLICE ALGORITHMS 101:
BINARY SEARCH TREES
Excerpt from Professor Drecker's Lecture

As we have seen in this lecture, we can use information about the structure of a binary search tree to search efficiently. Not only that, but we can add and remove nodes from trees. However, whenever we change a data structure, it is vitally important to ensure that we're not violating the properties that we use.

For binary search trees, it is important to maintain the *binary search tree property*. This property states that (1) the values of the data in the left node (and all its children) are less than or equal to the value of the current node and (2) the values of the data in the right node (and all its children) are greater than or equal to the value of the current node. If we violate this property, we no longer have a binary search tree, and we can't prune branches of the tree during a search.

Tries for Paperwork

After two searches through the full set of transfers, Frank still hadn't found anyone suspicious. More precisely, he hadn't found anyone who had any clear involvement in the plot. Frank was at least a little suspicious of everyone.

"Hey, Notation's in here," remarked Socks on their second pass through.

Frank sighed. "Of course she's in there, Socks. She just graduated from the academy. This is a ledger of officers from the academy."

"She did pretty well in school, didn't she?" asked Socks as he skimmed her transfer papers.

"Focus, Socks," said Frank. "Remember, we're looking for anything *suspicious*."

"Three recent graduates transferred to the castle," offered Socks. "Maybe we should look into one of them. Gretchen thinks—"

"No." Frank cut him off with a shake of his head. He'd already seen those transfers, and they were all completely clean. Between the three of them, there wasn't so much as a single citation for non-regulation-length toenails.

"There's nothing here," Frank said at last. As Socks began to protest, Frank cut him off again. "You should go back to my office. I'll meet you there after I brief the captain, and we can go over whatever leads are left."

Frank thought he saw a look of relief pass over Socks's face, but wasn't sure if he was just projecting it. He had known rookies to fake appendicitis to the point of actually going though with the surgery just to miss a single weekly briefing.

Instead of heading straight up to the captain's office, Frank returned to the record room. The captain had given him the official report, but Frank hadn't had a chance to investigate the scene of the crime himself. Maybe he'd get lucky and find a clue.

The record officer was a rookie by the name of John Cache who, after grudgingly allowing him into the room, trailed after Frank with a vigilant eye. Perhaps after the theft the station had tightened its security, though Cache's behavior was probably just due to rookie eagerness. Every rookie fantasizes about foiling crimes and saving the day on at least a weekly basis.

Under the pretense of looking for information about a lost dragon, Frank scanned the shelves of books. As expected for a station of this size, the volume of paperwork was enormous. Paperwork seemed to grow quadratically with the size of any government organization, and the capital police station had more officers than any other two stations combined. Even without the stolen scrolls, the room was packed full.

Luckily, the record officers kept the information well organized. As per the king's regulation *The Storage of Paperwork and Other Flat Work Products for Agencies of More Than 10 People*, every document was categorized and stored by subject. Large portions of shelves were dedicated to such topics as arrest reports, expense reports, transfers, guard rotations, and noise complaints.

The room itself was organized like a giant *trie*. Tries, also known as *prefix trees*, are data structures that allow efficient searches over sets of strings. Conceptually similar to binary search trees, tries start at a root node and branch out as they move down. However, tries are optimized for searching strings instead of numeric values. At each node, the trie splits the data based on the question "What is the *next* letter in the string?" Thus, each node in a trie can have many children, one for each letter in the alphabet. This structure lets you efficiently search for any string by following a single path down the trie, choosing the next node based solely on the next letter in your target string.

Frank had once seen a demonstration of a magic trie at a wizards' convention. The neon orange tree had hung in the air, storing the names of the thousand potion ingredients carried by that vendor. For simplicity, the trie showed only the non-empty branches. Customers could use the trie to quickly determine which ingredients were in stock. For example, they could see the vendor carried *batnip* by taking the B, A, T, N, I, then P branches. And they could quickly tell that *baby powder* was out of stock because the subtree under BA didn't have a branch corresponding to B.

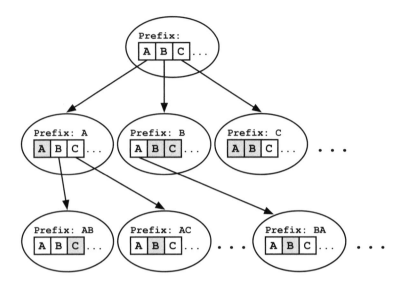

The record room took the concept of tries and applied it to shelving. Twenty-six massive bookshelves lined the walls, each holding records starting with a single letter. They were the trie's first level of nodes. First was the A shelf, followed by the B shelf, and so forth.

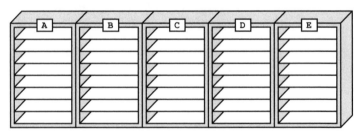

Next, each bookshelf contained individual shelves, each of which corresponded to the second letter of a subject. These shelves made up the trie's next layer.

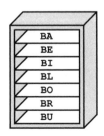

Because most two-letter combinations didn't correspond to existing entries, the bookshelves didn't need 26 individual shelves. Frank had heard stories of record officers killing time by inventing new subjects to fill the gaps. Apparently, a senior officer had received a long lecture from the captain on the seriousness of police work after she had suggested filing the speed limits under "Zoom policies." The Z bookcase still lacked a ZO shelf today.

The shelves were then arranged horizontally with labeled bookends representing the third level of the trie.

As he walked, Frank glanced over at the V shelf. During his time on the force, he had successfully lobbied to have the Vinettees occupy an entire subject of their own. He had spent many nights poring over the files in bookcase V, shelf I, section N.

Frank stopped at the D bookcase and located shelf R, section A. He pulled out a book on Dragon Registrations and pretended to skim it, while examining the rest of the room.

The captain's description of the crime had been accurate. Entire shelves of records had been swept clean, stripped of all scrolls corresponding to certain two-letter prefixes. Other bookcases were completely untouched. From his current vantage point, Frank could see empty shelves for the prefixes AS, CE, EX, NO, PR, and RO. He made a mental list of these prefixes. Whatever information the thief was after had those prefixes. And Frank had another lead.

He replaced the book on Dragon Registrations and announced loudly, "Good news! There are only a few Pigeon Eaters registered in the capital, and plenty of pigeons. At least the poor thing won't starve while I find it."

John Cache gave him a pitying look but said nothing as Frank strode from the records office.

POLICE ALGORITHMS **101:** TRIES
Excerpt from Professor Drecker's Lecture

Tries are tree-based data structures that allow the user to efficiently search for strings based on the string's prefix. Like binary search trees, tries start at a root node and branch out as they progress downward. In tries, each branching decision is based on the next element of the string. Thus, a node in a trie can have more than two children.

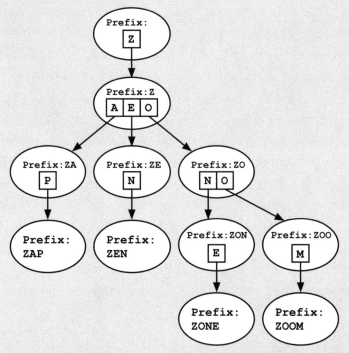

As with a binary tree, we only need to include nodes that have data. This example is constructed from the words *zap, zen, zone,* and *zoom.* Since we don't include *zonk,* we don't need to have a subtree under the K branch of ZON.

Note that we don't need to store the actual prefixes in the nodes; they can be reconstructed from the path through the tree. However, it can be useful to store one additional bit of information in each node: whether that node represents the end of a valid word. This allows us to distinguish between inserted words and prefixes of inserted words. For example, we could tell whether the word *zoo* had been inserted into a tree that also contains the word *zoom*.

Searching a trie is similar to searching a binary search tree. An algorithm starts at the top of the trie and progresses downward. At each node, the algorithm selects the branch corresponding to the next letter in the target string. For example, if we were searching for *zen*, we would follow the path from Z, through the branch for E, and then the branch for N.

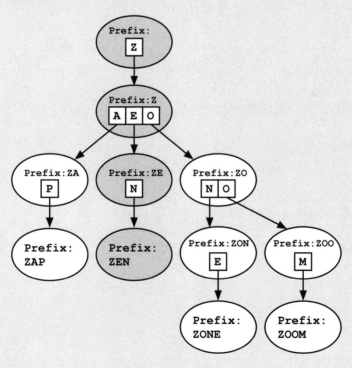

continued

If there is no such element, we know that the value of interest is not in the tree. So, if we were searching this tree for *zany*, we would hit a dead end after ZA.

One surprisingly common use of tries in policing is to compile a list of possible suspects. You'd be surprised by how frequently an informant refuses to provide a whole name, yet is comfortable providing the first few letters. In these cases, we can search the trie for that prefix and list all names in the corresponding subtree. Depending on the number and the rarity of the letters, this may be enough information to drastically limit the search.

Best-First Search: A Detective's Most Trusted Tool

Captain Donovan's office hadn't changed much in the last five years. The same desk sat in the center of the room, its surface clear aside from four baskets labeled "In," "Out," "To File," and "To Burn." A handful of new commendations adorned the wall, in addition to the large number Frank already recognized. Only the family pictures—charcoal sketches of the captain's two kids and a family portrait—gave any indication of the passage of time.

"Have a seat, Frank," said the captain without looking up from his paperwork.

Frank looked at the chairs in front of the captain's desk and thought back to the last time he'd sat in this office—his last day as a cop. He'd finally assembled enough evidence to go after Rebecca Vinettee yet again, even if some of his methods *had* bordered on dangerously randomized. The captain hadn't seen it the same way, though. His focus has been on Frank's blatant disregard for protocol rather than the new evidence. Pushing back the memory, Frank slumped into the right-hand chair and waited.

Finally, the captain signed the form, placed it in the "Out" basket, and met Frank's stare. "What've you found?"

"It's much bigger than a few missing files," Frank replied.

The captain looked unsurprised. "How big?"

Frank had spent the last hour playing out different versions of this meeting, weighing possible approaches. Ultimately he had decided to play to his strengths—and tact wasn't one of them.

"Why don't you start by telling me what you know?" said Frank. "What you really know, that is. No more lies. No more omissions."

The captain looked unfazed. "I never lied to you, Frank," he said. "I told you everything I knew when I came to see you." Frank started to object, but the captain held up his hand. "However, there have been additional developments since we spoke," he continued. "The most recent news reached me this morning."

"The other thefts?" asked Frank.

"Among other things," the captain said.

The captain leafed through his "Out" basket, retrieved a envelope labeled "Deliver to Frank Runtime," and handed it to Frank. "Here," he said. "We can save a runner the trip."

Frank opened the envelope and skimmed the papers. He found four incident reports—three detailing thefts at other police stations and a fourth detailing the attack on the military convoy. He'd known about the incidents, but the details took him by surprise.

"The Spell of Accelerated Rotting?" he asked.

"We called in wizards to confirm," said the captain. "The thieves rotted doors to the record rooms and pushed through."

"And the convoy?"

"Rotten crossbows," said the captain. "And one of the cart wheels—back left, I think. It should be in the report."

"What about the swords? The axes?"

"You never did bother to read the reports. The thieves also used the Spell of Accelerated Rusting. It's not particularly advanced magic, but it is effective."

"It doesn't say what they stole," Frank noted. "No mention of the mask."

The captain raised his eyebrows. "You know about the mask? That's highly classified."

Frank shrugged. "You're paying me to find information," he said, leaving out the fact that Socks had let this information slip only by accident. It never paid to let your clients know how much of your success was due to other people's stupidity.

"It's worrying, Frank," said the captain. "That's a powerful artifact. Add in the anonymous tip we received about a possible attack on the castle, and the whole force is on alert. We've had to pull people off other posts to step up security."

"I've heard the same thing about the castle," Frank admitted. He flipped through the documents once more. "No leads on the attackers?"

"We've heard some rumors, but nothing solid. At least nothing firm enough to put in a report."

"What about your officers?" asked Frank. "Do you have any suspects there?"

The captain studied him before responding. Frank knew the captain would never have come to him if he didn't suspect an inside job. But there was a substantial gap between a general flicker of suspicion and a short list of names.

"No," said the captain. "I haven't found anything yet. There's no common thread running through the thefts. Different stations. Different officers on duty. Even different departments."

Frank nodded silently while he turned the thefts over in his mind. He had hit the same dead end with the internal transfers. There had been at least one new transfer on duty for each incident, but never the same officer twice. Frank had briefly considered the possibility of a broad conspiracy throughout the entire rookie class, but discarded it immediately. Anyone capable of coordinating such a massive betrayal would likely have been able to orchestrate more subtle thefts, at least something that didn't involve alerting every station within a hundred miles.

"And Officer Notation?" Frank asked.

The captain looked genuinely taken aback. "What about her?"

"Is she on your list?" asked Frank.

"She was on duty that night, so she's on my list," he said. "But she's near the bottom. Notation's a good kid. She's green, but she's dedicated to the force."

"Did you know she's been investigating the theft herself?"

The captain frowned. "I suppose it shouldn't surprise me. As I said, she's dedicated. Where did you run into her?"

"Crannock's farm," said Frank. "She tagged along for a while after that."

"Did she now? And?"

"I don't trust her," said Frank.

"You don't trust anyone, Frank."

Frank sighed. "It's more than that," he said. "Just let me know if you notice anything strange."

"What about you?" prompted the captain. "What have you found?"

Frank proceeded to give him a quick summary. He told the captain how he had followed a tip to Crannock's farm and picked up a trail of clues that led him to Usb, the Vinettees ship, and Rebecca Vinettee.

At this news, the captain interrupted him with a chuckle. "Another run-in with the Vinettees, Frank? Rebecca too. I'm surprised you're still walking around. How many of them have you put behind bars?"

"Not enough," Frank said.

"Fair," conceded the captain. "How'd you get out of there?"

"A wizard showed up and started flinging barrels of pickled eels," Frank said as though this were a perfectly normal occurrence.

The captain gaped at him. "What?"

"A junior wizard by the name of Socks," Frank explained. "He's an apprentice to a wizard named Gretchen. Apparently the king brought in a few senior wizards to help with the case."

"I can't say that I've ever heard of Gretchen, but it doesn't surprise me that the king brought the wizards in," said the captain. "After the attack on the convoy, the king has mobilized everyone he can. Even Princess Ann is returning from her latest quest. She arrives back at the castle tomorrow."

That single sentence spoke volumes as to the severity of the situation. Princess Ann was almost constantly away leading missions, quests, or critical negotiations. For her to return, the situation must be bad.

"Princess Ann is coming back?" asked Frank.

"She thinks this recent attack might be related to the League of Unnecessary Complexity."

"The League of Unnecessary Complexity?"

"It all comes back to the evil wizard, Exponentious," explained the captain. "You know, the one who tried to destroy the kingdom."

Frank nodded. He clearly remembered the terror that had swept through the kingdom when Exponentious attacked. These days, the tale of his campaign was told in hushed voices around the campfire to scare junior wizards and knights.

The captain continued, "He's been safely locked away in the royal prison since then, but Princess Ann is worried that he wasn't acting alone. That maybe he had followers, accomplices, admirers, something like that. She's been tracking clues about this mysterious new league of wizards apparently bent on destroying the kingdom. So far they've been staying in the shadows, conducting only small attacks. But the royal family is worried."

Frank stared blankly at the captain. Could this be the same league mentioned by the Vinettee thug on the *Retry Loop*? If so, what had he gotten himself into? Then another thought struck him.

"The attack on the castle! Could it have anything to do with Princess Ann's return?" Frank asked. "If she's been out hunting this League of Unnecessary Complexity, they could be looking to strike back."

"We've thought about that," agreed the captain. "We'll be pulling another hundred officers into guard duty when she returns. It'll leave the armory, prison, and police stations low. But we can't take a chance."

"What about the mask? Someone could use that to infiltrate the guards."

"Yes, it's a perfect opportunity to sneak into the castle," the captain acknowledged. "Even without the mask, adding a hundred new guards makes it almost impossible to recognize everyone. But we're taking precautions. The royal wizard Marcus created magic identification badges for the castle guards. They are almost impossible to fake, and they flash bright red if the wearer doesn't match the name or the picture."

Frank's mind raced as he searched for another hole in the security.

"Go on," prompted the captain. "What else did you find?"

Frank sped up, racing through their day on the *TCP Flyer* and their search of Mudwall and Frayed Cable Island. He described the attack in the prison and the loss of the documents. Finally, he detailed the recent leads from the threads and transfer logs.

"Which is why you want to know about Notation," said the captain. "She's a recent transfer from the academy."

"It's one of the reasons," admitted Frank. "Her name came up in my range search."

The captain thought about this for a moment, then said, "I don't think she's the type. My gut says she's a good officer. But I'm not sure who to trust right now. She shouldn't be working the case anyway. It's not her assignment."

"Thank you," Frank said.

"Any other transfers I should look into?"

Frank shook his head. "Some of the rookies were at the various crime scenes, but there's no common thread. No one could have been involved in more than one theft. So unless you have a whole class of traitors, I think it's a dead end."

"That's good work, Frank," said the captain. "One of the nicest examples of best-first search I've seen in years."

Frank smiled. Even within the force, few people would bother to refer to this type of investigation as best-first search. More often, a person would say "I'm looking into things" or "I'm following up on some leads."

Despite this lack of recognition, best-first search was a staple for every police officer, ranking up there with other vital tools like a notebook and a pair of comfortable shoes. In best-first search, you kept a list of current leads, picked the most promising one to follow, and followed it. Once you had followed that lead, you simply picked the next best one to follow. Any new clues found along the way were added to the list. It was the single best tool to solve many cases.

"Anything else?" asked the captain.

Frank shook his head.

"All right," said the captain. "Keep at it then. If the League of Unnecessary Complexity really does exist and is behind this, then we're in a lot deeper than I thought. You better watch your back, Frank."

"I always do," Frank replied. He started to stand, but paused. "One more question. Do you know how Notation knew about the ArrayCart?"

"I don't," said the captain, now looking past Frank. "Why don't we ask her? It looks like she's standing outside my office at this very moment."

POLICE ALGORITHMS 101: BEST-FIRST SEARCH
Excerpt from Professor Drecker's Lecture

If you remember only one algorithm from this course, it should be best-first search. This algorithm will be your best tool on the force. You will need it on every case. And, of course, it will be on the final.

Best-first search is an algorithm that chooses the next state to explore based on a score or score function. Each newly discovered search state is given a score that corresponds to how good the algorithm believes it to be. For example, you might label states by their probability of containing the target value (if you can estimate it) or the quality of a lead in an investigation. At each step, the algorithm chooses to explore the state with the highest score. You can visualize the operation of best-first search as keeping a *sorted* list of states to try next.

Best-first search can also be used to minimize the costs associated with each state, such as the estimated distance of the state to the goal. In this case, the algorithm chooses the next state by which one most minimizes the cost.

Consider a very simple maze where you know the coordinates of the start and the goal locations. You can label each state in the search space with a cost equal to the distance from that state to the goal. For example, you could use the *Manhattan distance*—the total vertical distance to the goal plus the total horizontal distance to the goal. This label doesn't necessarily mean that this state will get you there, but it does provide a signal for the search algorithm.

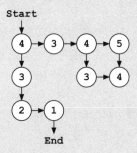

As the search progresses, it will explore different states (shown as shaded circles), find new unexplored states, and add the unexplored states to the list of states to try (enclosed in dashed circles). In each iteration, the search selects the best unexplored state according to the score or cost. In this example, this means selecting the state with the smallest cost.

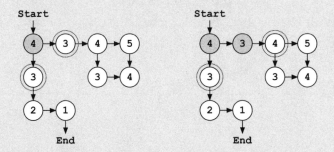

continued

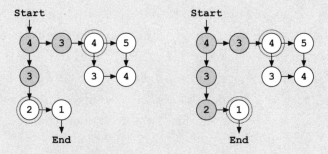

We can terminate the search as soon as we find the end state. In this example, we only need to explore a little over half the states. For example, we never chose to explore the second state of distance 4, because we always had a better option to try first.

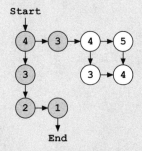

When you're in the field, you'll have to determine how to prioritize leads. Depending on the case, you might want to start with the freshest leads or the most concrete information. Regardless, you should always be prioritizing your search.

—24—
Priority Queues for Investigations

C aptain Donavan," Notation blurted as she came into the office. "I'd like to personally apologize for conducting an unauthorized investigation outside of working hours. But this is *my* investigation as much as Frank's, and if he's briefing—"

"And how exactly did it become *your* investigation, Officer Notation?" interrupted the captain. "I thought I had assigned you to the counterfeit yo-yo case. Why were you at Crannock's farm investigating stolen papers?"

"I was following a lead—" started Notation.

"You were following a lead?" interrupted the captain. "I didn't see anything about an ArrayCart in any of your reports."

"It occurred to me that morning," explained Notation.

"You decided to pursue this lead instead of reporting it to the detective in charge of the investigation?"

Frank winced. The captain was obsessed with following the correct protocol for an investigation. On the captain's personal list of horrendous violations, the failure to report a lead ranked somewhere above the use of heuristic data structures and right under the refusal to shower. From Notation's near-panicked expression, he could tell she was thinking the same thing.

"I was already near the farm," she said. "And—"

"What was the lead?" asked Frank.

Notation turned to him in surprise, either horror-struck that he'd interrupted the captain's interrogation or because she'd simply forgotten he was there.

"I remembered something from the night of the theft," she said. "I'd just finished my nightly report when I saw an odd cart out the window. I didn't think anything of it at the time, because the fishmongers are always using strange carts. I figured it was the morning eel delivery."

She turned to the captain, her eyes pleading. "It seemed like such a long shot," she explained. "I figured it would be a dead end, that the cart was just a delivery. I didn't want to report it until I knew more."

"And then you joined Frank on the investigation for almost two full days," said the captain.

"We'd found some promising leads," offered Notation.

"Officer Notation," the captain snapped. "I don't care if you were being led by the ghost of a former police captain. Procedures exist for a reason. You didn't follow them."

Notation stared hard at the ground. "I understand, sir."

"No," said the captain. "I'm not sure you do. But you'll have plenty of time to think about it. You're on desk duty until further notice."

Notation shuddered, but didn't protest.

The captain turned to Frank. "And you have work to do, Frank," he said, ending the meeting.

As she turned to leave, Notation's eyes fixed on the portrait of King Fredrick hanging on the wall. She seemed lost in thought for a moment.

"Captain," she said suddenly. "Do you have any priority queues?"

Frank took a moment to make the connection, but finally dredged up the faint memory. One of his professors had droned on in class about how King Fredrick had popularized priority queues.

Before he'd become king, Fredrick held audience to hear the complaints and concerns of the kingdom's citizens. Due to his tight schedule and the abundance of the citizenry's complaints, he had been forced to develop a prioritization scheme. A prince could only be expected to endure so many complaints at a time.

First Prince Fredrick had tried a complaint stack, hearing the most recent complaints first, but then he missed important older complaints. Then he tried a complaint queue, hearing the oldest complaints first, but then he missed important recent complaints. Finally, he'd employed a new data structure—the priority queue— which allowed him to hear the most important complaints first.

"Priority queues?" asked the captain, clearly thrown off by the sudden question. Almost nobody dared speak following a lecture from the captain. They simply shuffled humbly out of the office or, in some cases, spent the next few hours huddled in a dark broom closet.

"Data structures," explained Notation, apparently on autopilot. "They're like regular queues: you enqueue and dequeue items. But they also require each item to have a priority score—a measure of importance. When you dequeue an item, the priority queue always gives you the next most important item."

Seeing blank stares from both the captain and Frank, Notation pressed on with an example. "If I inserted four items, with priorities 1, 2, 4, and 3, I would extract them in the order 4, 3, 2, 1."

"I know what priority queues are," said the captain. "We use them for storing the list of noise complaints. The louder noises get higher priority, so we are always addressing the worst cases first. I heard they use them for smell complaints near the sewage marshes as well. Although it seems like everything there would have an equally high priority—unbearable. But what's your point?

"Do you have any?" Notation asked.

The captain shook his head, confusion still keeping his anger in check. "None to spare," he said. "We're using all of the priority queues we have—one for noise complaints, three for different types of crimes, one for the most wanted list, and one for vacation requests. Why?"

"Best-first search," said Notation.

"Best-first search?" asked the Captain. "Frank told me that he was already using best-first search."

"That's right," confirmed Frank.

"A priority queue would make it more efficient," explained Notation. "Each time we find a new lead, we could put it into the priority queue with a score indicating how good a lead it is. Then, when we're ready to explore the next lead, we take one off the priority queue. We'll always get the next best lead."

Frank sighed and shook his head. He knew the captain well enough to see how this was going to go. The captain excelled at his own brand of teaching moments. He wouldn't yell or curse, but would calmly lead a new officer into realizing their own stupidity. "How were you doing it before?" asked the captain in a patient tone. This was not going to end well.

"I keep the leads in a notebook," responded Notation. "Each time we're ready to explore a new lead, I scan through the entire list of leads to find the best one."

"And how many leads did you have?" asked the captain. "Let's say on average."

"On average?" Notation thought about this for a moment. "Between two and five, I guess."

"You want me to use one of the department's priority queues to help you scan through a list of two to five elements?" If the captain had used his customary growl, the question might have sounded less harsh. Instead, his calm patience made it excruciatingly clear how idiotic he found the whole discussion.

Notation flushed. "Well, priority queues aren't that expensive . . ." she started, but trailed off.

"Look, Officer Notation," said the captain. "I agree that priority queues are great for best-first search. After this meeting, I may order a whole new set, one for each detective. But you don't need one right now. To start with, you don't have enough leads. More importantly, *you aren't even on this case.*"

Notation's face had reddened progressively throughout the lecture, and it had now achieved the complexion of beet soup. She took a deep breath, looked the captain straight in the eye, and mumbled, "I understand, sir."

Frank felt a surge of pity. Notation had made a classic rookie mistake, overoptimizing the solution. He had to hand it to her—the idea of using priority queues for tracking leads was perfectly reasonable. In fact, he'd been using a priority queue this entire time. However, her timing on the question couldn't have been worse.

"Notation," the captain continued, "you've got a lot of promise here. You're bright, you're driven, and you have good instincts. But you have to learn to follow orders. Don't end up like Frank here."

Notation opened her mouth as though to protest. Then she glanced at Frank, grimaced, and closed her mouth without a word of argument. She nodded curtly, snapped a salute, and strode from the office.

"And you, Frank, have work to do. Get going."

Frank turned and followed Notation out, not bothering with even a nod.

Frank waited until they had reached the stairs before speaking.

"You know . . . there's a wizard in the Orb district that can make you an inexpensive priority queue. His name is Heaperous, actually. I think that's how he got into data structures in the first place. With a name like Heaperous, I suppose it's an inevitability. Anyway, the priority queue won't be pretty, but it'll work. He only works mornings, though, so you'll have to wait 'til tomorrow."

Notation stopped walking and gave him a suspicious look. "Why are you telling me this, Frank?"

Frank forced his face into his best sympathetic look. "I've been on the receiving end of many of the captain's speeches. And, more importantly, I know how valuable a good data structure can be during an investigation."

"If good data structures are so valuable, then why don't *you* use a priority queue?" she shot back.

Frank shot her an irritated look. "Of course I use a priority queue. I've been using one since we started. Did you think I've been keeping all the clues in my head? I'm too old for that sort of thing."

"What?" exclaimed Notation. "You've been using a priority queue this whole time? Why didn't you say anything to the captain?"

Frank laughed at this. "You have a lot to learn about the captain, rookie. First off, you never interrupt him while he's ranting about *anything*. I once saw a detective put on desk duty for a month because she derailed a rant about tofu. It wasn't even a particularly good rant. He'd got stuck alternating between its squishy texture and its lack of taste."

Notation stared at Frank, apparently at a loss for words.

"The point is," Frank continued, "sometimes you need to take matters into your own hands. If a priority queue will help you, don't wait for the requisition process. Just go out and buy one."

Notation considered this advice. Finally, she nodded. "I guess that buying my own equipment won't technically violate any policies. Thank you, Frank."

The excitement on Notation's face almost made Frank feel guilty. Any wizard shop in town could make a priority queue, and most would match Heaperous's prices. But Heaperous's shop in the Orb district was the farthest one still within city limits, and Frank needed to make sure Notation stayed out the way for a little while longer.

POLICE ALGORITHMS 101: PRIORITY QUEUES
Excerpt from Professor Drecker's Lecture

Of all the data structures you'll encounter during your career in the police force, I guarantee that priority queues will be the most valuable. Like stacks and queues, priority queues are data structures that allow you to insert data and later remove it in a specific order. Where stacks and queues enforce orderings determined by when an element was inserted, priority queues order the data by decreasing priority. The next element removed is the highest-priority element in the queue, regardless of when it was inserted.

Each item inserted into a priority queue must also have a priority, or score. This could be the value of the element itself or a value computed by a different function.

continued

Consider this example of prioritizing noise complaints based on their severity. If you inserted the complaints in the following order:

> "The crowd at the Exponentiated Expresso"
> (score = 3)
> "Crab's Pinch sea shanty contest" (score = 6)
> "Farmer Swinson's rabbit" (score = 1)
> "Farmer Swinson's rooster" (score = 5)
> "Farmer Swinson" (score = 7)

You would retrieve them from the priority queue as:

> "Farmer Swinson" (score = 7)
> "Crab's Pinch sea shanty contest" (score = 6)
> "Farmer Swinson's rooster" (score = 5)
> "The crowd at the Exponentiated Expresso"
> (score = 3)
> "Farmer Swinson's rabbit" (score = 1)

Note that there are no guarantees that the data will be sorted within the priority queue, only that it is extracted in order. As you'll see in later lectures, data structures called *heaps* are an efficient way of implementing priority queues that do *not* keep the data in fully sorted order.

The capital's station uses a variety of priority functions. As you might expect, the queue most hotly debated is the vacation priority queue. This queue is ordered solely by the officer's number of unused vacation days. Despite previous requests, no additional priority is given for the niceness of the vacation spot. Upcoming trips to glaciers, beaches, and swamps are treated equally. Instead, the queue prioritizes based on one measure of fairness. It helps to ensure that the next officer to go on vacation is the one who's taken the fewest vacation days this year.

Priority Queues for Lock Picking

A small group of thugs was waiting outside the door to Frank's office. They were trying to blend in, but Frank spotted them a block away. One sat on a bench, pretending to read a paper while his eyes darted around the street. Three others stood near the corner, arguing loudly about a recent sporting match. As he neared, Frank realized they were discussing completely different sports. One thug ranted about the officiating at the last royal polo match, another interjected with tips about an upcoming horse race, and the third seemed content with just saying the word "sports" at regular intervals.

Only the spy succeeded in being inconspicuous. She was waiting across the street, where she leaned casually against the wall. If he hadn't chased her earlier, Frank might have completely overlooked her. She was good. Or, more accurately, the thugs were really bad.

Without breaking stride, Frank turned and started down a side street. He couldn't go back to the office, not with a contingent of Vinettee thugs waiting for him. After a moment's thought, he settled on an old police safe house. It was close and hadn't been used in years. If he was lucky, he might even remember the combination to the lock.

Frank made it half a block before he heard the shouts and pounding footsteps behind him. The spy must have alerted the others.

"Frank!" yelled one particularly beefy thug. "We just want to talk."

As if this claim weren't far-fetched enough, the laughter from the rest of the thugs dispelled any doubt about their intentions. Frank broke into a run. The footsteps behind him followed suit.

Frank cut left sharply, heading into a narrow alley. He knew this part of town well and was sure he could lose his pursuers. He just had to buy himself enough time to get into the safe house. Getting in could take a while, unless he remembered the combination on the first try.

Frank emerged from the alley onto Flag Street and pulled a quick U-turn, heading into the store on the corner. He pretended to peruse the racks of baby clothes while watching through the window. The rack of Tike's Tunics provided an ideal vantage point.

Within a minute, the thugs spilled out onto the street and stood around, looking confused. The spy followed and began shouting orders. She split the thugs into two groups and sent them down the street in both directions—one group on each side—while she waited at the mouth of the alley.

Frank didn't waste any time. He hurried through the shop and exited through a back door that led into the alley. The spy stood only 10 feet away, her back to Frank. As quietly as he could, Frank retreated down the alley and made his way to the safe house. If he was lucky and the thugs didn't think to ask the shopkeeper about him, he had bought some time.

At the safe house door, Frank fumbled with the combination lock. He spun the dial to 1, around to 1, and finally back around to 1 again. Admittedly, it was a simple code. The lock didn't open.

Frank swore. Someone must have changed the combination since he'd last been here. He considered his options. He could try to find the combination, which might take him a long time, or he could find another place to hide. Unable to think of anywhere safe that didn't take him past the thugs again, he turned back to the lock.

Since time was short, Frank needed to be efficient. The lock required three numbers, each 1–20, so he faced 8,000 possible combinations. He didn't have time for a breadth-first search or a depth-first search. Instead he would have to rely on a limited best-first search and some liberal guessing; he would have to trust his gut. He withdrew his priority queue from his pocket, wiped it clean, and started jotting down combinations. With each combination, he added a priority—how likely he felt it would be. He started with some common police combinations:

1-2-3

1-1-2

1-3-5

He gave each of those a priority of 10.

Then he moved on to other triples of the same number. If the code had once been 1-1-1, why not use 2-2-2? The safe houses were used rarely enough that it paid to keep the combinations simple. He listed 19 untried triplets, giving them priorities of 5. The priority queue now held 22 possibilities.

Then he quickly ran through the birthdays of the officers responsible for the safe houses. That added another 6 combinations, which he assigned priorities of 8. He added the birthdays of every other officer he could remember, dropping the priority to 2 for those.

Finally he added the word *RUN* and assigned it a priority of 1. He knew full well that if he reached that option, it was time to give up. He would have to find another place to hide.

The priority queue now held 32 options. The result was a long list of possible combinations to try. At the top was the highest-priority combination, 1-2-3. Frank tried it, but nothing happened.

He swore and removed the combination from the priority queue. A new highest-priority combination popped to the top.

Before he could try the next combination, a thought struck him. Maybe they used some variation of the old combination? He had known plenty of officers to use one combination for their locker and its reverse for their luggage. Could the officer in charge of the safe houses have done something similar here? Frank added 3-2-1 to the bottom of his list with a priority of 9.

Neither 1-1-2 or 1-3-5 worked, which exhausted all of the priority-10 combinations. Frank crossed them off and added their reversed combinations, 2-1-1 and 5-3-1, to the bottom of the list. Again he used priority 9, figuring that a reversed combination would be easy for people to remember.

He read the next-highest-priority combination, 3-2-1, from the top of the list. It was one of the reversed combinations he had recently added. That was the magic of priority queues: no matter what order you added the items, you always got the best entry next.

The lock finally clicked open at 5-3-1, one of the priority-9 codes he'd added. Frank breathed a sigh of relief and glanced around. Still no sign of the Vinettees. He was safe for now.

POLICE ALGORITHMS 101:
DATA STRUCTURES AND SEARCH
Excerpt from Professor Drecker's Lecture

As we've discussed in lectures throughout the semester, the data structures we use can impact both how an algorithm functions and how efficient it is. During the lectures on depth-first search and breadth-first search, we looked at how the difference between stacks and queues impacted the search order. The use of priority queues for best-first search is another great example of the impact of data structures.

Conceptually, best-first search is similar to both breadth-first and depth-first search. At each step in the algorithm, we are choosing a single new state to explore. The key difference is how we order our exploration of new states. Using a priority queue allows us to efficiently pick *the most promising* next state. Best-first search and priority queues are perfect complements and make an extremely efficient data structure–algorithm combination.

—26—
Heuristics in Search

Frank spent the night alternately reviewing clues, watching out the windows for Vinettee thugs, and bemoaning the safe house's lack of food. Soon, he realized that it wasn't just food that was missing. The apartment lacked the standard equipment—blank notebooks, quills, and sturdy furniture—found in every police building. Once he thought to look for it, Frank quickly located a large "For Rent" sign in the window. He was just lucky the police hadn't rented it out or changed the combination yet.

After a few hours, Frank convinced himself the Vinettees wouldn't find him. He abandoned the windows, began to pace the empty apartment, and focused on the case. The When and Where were easy—the clues suggested an attack on the castle tomorrow night. Unfortunately, aside from the When and Where, Frank still didn't have any answers. In particular, the Who, Why, How, and Could-I-Sneak-Out-for-Food-Without-the-Vinettees-Seeing-Me remained important open questions.

After an hour of pacing while trying to fill in the remaining details, Frank had started to doubt even the When and Where. An attack on the castle seemed too obvious, and the police were already prepared for it. Even Socks was telling everyone he knew to watch for it.

Frank stopped and swore as realization dawned. Socks had to be involved. With a familiar sense of *I knew I shouldn't trust anyone*, Frank replayed the events of the last few days in his mind, this time recognizing the signs. He should have seen it when Socks's staff "accidentally" ignited the papers in the cell and destroyed the evidence. He should have realized that someone had tipped off the spy about his visit to the cloak shop. He should have at least wondered about the absurd and conveniently timed rescue with the barrels of pickled eels. But above all else, he should have been absolutely certain from the moment Socks incorrectly inserted a node into the binary tree. No expert in binary trees would ever make that mistake by accident. It was true that he'd been suspicious the whole time, but then again, Frank suspected everyone all the time.

The realization left him with even more questions. The Where and When were unanswered again. If Socks had been feeding them false information, Frank had to question everything. What were the wizards going to do, and how were they going to do it? Knowing the Why would also be nice, but Frank found that whenever he foiled elaborate plots, the perpetrators tended to babble on about the Why without provocation. By this point, he'd also given up on sneaking out for food, closing that question for now with a growling stomach.

"How does the mask fit in?" Frank muttered to himself. If the thieves were planning to attack the castle, could they still use the mask? Or would Marcus's ID badges render it useless? Did they just need it to break into the police station? And what records were the thieves after? Frank started enumerating the questions in his notebook. They quickly outnumbered the clues.

Frank thought about his next step. With such a limited timeline, he needed to push far into the realm of *heuristics*—rules of thumb that point algorithms in the right direction. For example, when searching for a lost turtle, Frank used the common "Check nearby first" heuristic, because turtles are slow. When seeking the freshest pot of coffee in the station, he relied on "Check the fullest cauldron" because it was often the most recently made. And when navigating to a tall castle in an unknown city, "Walk in the direction of the castle first" had usually gotten him there after only a few dead ends. Heuristics weren't perfect, but they provided useful information.

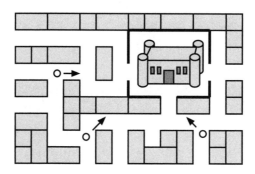

During his time on the police force, Frank had come to trust one heuristic above all others: follow the most concrete clues first. Specific names and physical evidence always trumped general suspicions and rumors.

It was a heuristic Frank had ignored only once in his career, when Glass Box Billy had provided multiple tips regarding an upcoming robbery. First, Billy had told Frank the getaway cart's exact waiting location, model, and pitch of wheel squeak. Second, Billy had relayed a rumor, overheard between bouts of raucous cheering at a game of darts, that Rebecca Vinettee was personally involved and the target had something to do with fish.

Frank had ignored every good police algorithm and decided to go after Rebecca Vinettee directly. He knew that she would disappear before they loaded the cart, probably using an alternate route back to the hideout. He had to catch her before she could vanish. He staked out the capital's Fish Depot, which was only two blocks from the getaway cart's location.

As the captain would later explain with excessively loud shouting, the Fish Depot happened to be two blocks in the wrong direction. On the other hand, the Orb Emporium was only a quarter of a block away from the getaway cart. A gang completely unaffiliated with the Vinettees stole 64 high-quality spherical glass orbs and 2 prototype cubic orbs, loaded them onto the getaway cart, and drove away with wheels squeaking precisely as annoyingly as Glass Box Billy had indicated. Frank's description of Billy's tip, and his insistence on adding a new heuristic of "always suspect the Vinettees," did not convince the captain.

In the current case, however, Frank was running out of even vague clues. He'd exhausted most of his concrete leads and was well into the realm of speculation and suspicion. If he wanted to make any more progress, he would need more information. He turned to his second most trusted heuristic: when at a dead end, collect more information. He needed to know more about the mask, how it could be used, and what magical defenses could thwart it. In this case, that meant finding an expert.

POLICE ALGORITHMS **101**: HEURISTICS
Excerpt from Professor Drecker's Lecture

Heuristics are rules of thumb that help point algorithms in the right direction. While you'll undoubtedly hear some officers dismiss heuristics as random guesses, you'll also see those same officers fall back on techniques and rules of thumb that have served them well in the past. It's important to realize that heuristics, like all information, are of varying quality.

One of the clearest examples of heuristics is navigating in the physical world. Whether you're wandering through a maze, searching an unknown city, or simply finding your way to the mess hall, you'll find yourself using heuristics to guide your search. Given two paths, which do you try first? A common and often reliable heuristic is to prioritize options according to simplified distance measures. My favorite is to use "as the bird flies" distance: How far away is the goal if there's nothing in your way? In practice, this heuristic means I always take the path that looks like it is getting me closer to the goal—the path that at least starts out in the correct direction. I might run into a few dead ends this way, but overall I've found this to be a good heuristic.

Of course, there are plenty of terrible heuristics as well. Officers who use new heuristics without properly vetting them can find themselves in deep trouble. A few years ago, a young officer created a particularly bad heuristic. After unprecedented success busting a smuggling ring, he got it into his head that all investigations must start at the docks. The problem was that this heuristic is wrong. It didn't help

continued

point his investigations in the right direction. In fact, it often led him immediately to a dead end. After 18 failed investigations, his captain assigned him to permanently patrolling the docks.

Heuristics shouldn't be random guesses. They need to contain some amount of useful information and be tailored to the correct problem.

Heaps in Politics and Academia

Early the next morning, Frank snuck out of the safe house and made his way across town to the police academy. Once on campus, surrounded by police officers, cadets, and retired officers, he felt himself relax. He even smiled broadly as he cut across the quad to the academy's faculty office building.

Frank hadn't been in the building in years. As a rule, the professors maintained an open-door policy that allowed students to stop by with questions anytime. In reality, few students ever took advantage of this access, preferring instead to wait until the night before a test to realize how much they didn't know. Frank often held out longer, waiting until he sat down to take the exam before realizing his ignorance.

A quick scan of the faculty directory indicated that Dr. Loop occupied the sole office on the building's top floor. Frank wasn't surprised. The peculiar design of the faculty building made office assignments a contentious topic in the best of times. Each floor held exactly half the offices of the floor beneath it, meaning that not only were the views better as you went up, but each office doubled in size. After years of bitter fighting, the dean had imposed a strict tenure-based priority for offices—the occupant of any office must have served a longer tenure than anyone in the offices directly below. In effect, he had turned the faculty building into a large tenure-based heap.

70							
40				61			
11		30		35		52	
10	8	22	18	11	5	12	

Dr. Olivia Loop, Professor of Wizard Criminology, had taught at the police academy for 70 years. Only Dr. Babbleton, Professor of Floating-Point Operations, came close to matching her tenure, at 61 years.

By the time Frank reached the top floor, he was breathing hard and wondering how a 95-year-old professor managed that climb multiple times a day. Then again, she did have the benefit of constant exercise.

"Come in, come in," called Dr. Loop through her open door. "Have a seat before you fall down. Those stairs can be tough, even for a youngster like you."

Frank entered the office and slumped gratefully into one of the hard wooden chairs in front of Dr. Loop's desk. He struggled for breath for another moment as Dr. Loop watched him silently.

"Nice office," Frank finally managed.

"It *is* wonderful, isn't it?" said Dr. Loop. "I had to wait 70 years to make it here—70 years! Professor Iterator simply refused to retire for the longest time. But I just waited patiently. You know what happened the day Professor Iterator called it quits?"

Frank shook his head, still too winded to give a proper response.

"That young upstart, Dr. Lambda, tried to steal my office!"

"Really?" Frank wheezed.

Dr. Loop shrugged. "You know how it is. Retirement at the police academy is always an exciting affair. Due to our tenure system, only the most senior professor can put in for retirement. Once that happens, no one can resist the chance to sneak into a better office.

"Honestly, it was all Professor Iterator's fault. After 75 years, he just packed up and stormed out, muttering about troublesome kids. As per tradition, the only person he told was the one nearest the door—Dr. Lambda, who has been here only 11 years.

75							
70				61			
40		30		35		52	
10	8	22	18	11	5	12	11

"Not caring about our well-established system for office assignments, Dr. Lambda packed the contents of his meager office and moved straight up here. Ha! It happens every time someone leaves. The professor with the very last office in the entire building runs upstairs and tries to take the top office. Every single time, I tell you!

11							
70				61			
40		30		35		52	
10	8	22	18	11	5	12	

"Of course, once I heard of Dr. Iterator's departure, I raced right up here to claim the office for myself. It was rightfully mine, you see. I had the only legitimate claim, having been here for 70 years. But Dr. Babbleton heard me running up the stairs and decided to try for it as well. It always happens like that, you know.

11							
70				61			
40		30		35		52	
10	8	22	18	11	5	12	

"Once an office opens up, both the professors who live below it rush up to make a claim. Unless a grant application is due—then it can take a few weeks for anyone to notice. In this case, Dr. Babbleton and I also had to contend with Dr. Lambda's predictable attempt to get the best office.

"Anyway, there we were—Dr. Lambda, Dr. Babbleton, and me. We argued for a good hour about the tenure rules. Dr. Lambda had no claim and we all knew it, but he stubbornly held his ground for a while. The argument really came down to Dr. Babbleton, who had been here a paltry 61 years, and me. Inevitably, I won out—forcing Dr. Lambda to move down into my old room. Dr. Babbleton remained in her office on the floor below.

11							
70				61			
40		30		35		52	
10	8	22	18	11	5	12	

"Dr. Lambda packed up his belongings and moved to my office, but the poor man found two other professors already waiting there. They had occupied the office below mine and were looking for an opportunity to upgrade.

70						
11		61				
40	**30**	35		52		
10	8	22	18	11	5	12

"They both had better claims on my old office, one having been here 30 years and the other 40. This time, Dr. Lambda didn't put up much of a fight. Dr. Variable won that office. He deserved it, too, after 40 years.

70						
↗11		61				
40↙	**30**	35		52		
10	8	22	18	11	5	12

"As luck would have it, Dr. Lambda finally caught a break on the next floor down. There the two professors below were both more junior than Dr. Lambda. I think he took particular pleasure in claiming victory and shutting the door in their faces.

70						
40		61				
11	30	35		52		
10	**8**	22	18	11	5	12

"In a way, Dr. Lambda was lucky," explained Dr. Loop. "When he tried to steal the top office, he ended up on the other side of the building with more junior professors. He got to move up a whole floor. The rules only state that the occupant of any office must have served a longer tenure than anyone in the offices *directly* below. So, by pure luck, Dr. Lambda now has an office on the second floor while some of his more senior colleagues are still on the first floor."

Frank waited politely to see if the story would continue. When it didn't, he ventured, "Dr. Loop, if I could have a moment of your time? I have a few questions."

"Of course," said Dr. Loop. "I assume this is about this week's assignment?"

Frank balked, thrown off in mid-thought. "What? No. I'm not a student here."

"You aren't? Then you should consider the police force. It's a noble career."

"I graduated over 10 years ago."

"Is that so?" Dr. Loop shrugged again. "After a while, all the kids just blend together."

"Okay," Frank said, desperately trying to regain his train of thought. "Right. I need to know about security spells."

"Oh, I don't *teach* magic," explained Dr. Loop. "I teach Wizard Criminology, it's the study of—"

"I took your class," Frank interrupted. "I don't want to know how to perform spells. I want to know what types of security spells exist. Particularly in police stations."

Dr. Loop's expression suddenly grew hard. "That's very sensitive information," she said, her voice cold. "Known only to a few people."

"That's why I'm here," said Frank.

"Why, exactly, do you need this information?" she asked.

"I'm investigating a theft at the Capital Police Station," he shot back. First the blathering story, now she was grilling him? He didn't have time for this.

"I will need to see your badge," prompted Dr. Loop. She made a beckoning motion with her hand.

Frank reached into his trench cloak and retrieved his Private Investigator badge. He tossed it on her desk.

"A PI?" Dr. Loop laughed. Then, her voice grew hard again. "Get out of my office."

"Doctor Loop—" started Frank, but stopped at the sound of a crossbow being cocked.

POLICE ALGORITHMS **101:** HEAPS
Excerpt from Professor Drecker's Lecture

A *max heap* is a binary tree–based data structure that maintains a special ordered relationship between a node and its children. Specifically, a heap stores the elements according to the *heap property*, which for a max heap states that the value at any node in the tree is larger (or equal to) every element below it. This structure allows the max heap to efficiently support several important operations: (1) efficiently finding the largest element, (2) removing the largest element, and (3) inserting an arbitrary element. These three operations make heaps ideal data structures for implementing priority queues.

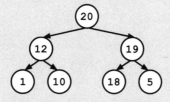

Heaps are often visualized as trees, though they're easy to implement as arrays, where each element in the array corresponds to a node in the tree, with the root node at index 0, as shown in the following diagram. Child node indexes are defined relative to the indexes of their parents. Specifically, a node at index i has children at indexes $2i + 1$ and $2i + 2$. So the node at index 1 will have a child at index $(2 \times 1) + 1 = 3$, and at $(2 \times 1) + 2 = 4$, as shown in the diagram.

continued

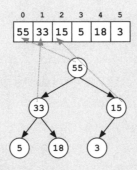

Alternatively, some heap implementations just skip array index 0 for simplicity. The root node is instead placed at index 1. In this case, a node at index i has children at indexes $2i$ and $2i + 1$, making the index computations simpler. Either way, the indexing scheme allows the algorithm to compute the index of a child based on the parent, and a parent based on the child.

Since the root node (the first element in the array) always corresponds to the maximum value in a max heap, you can always find this value in constant time (that is, in the same amount of time no matter how many values are in the array). This allows a user to efficiently look up the highest-valued item on the priority queue.

If you want to add an element or remove the max element, the processes are more complicated, as they require first breaking and then restoring the heap property.

You add a new element to the heap by first appending it to the back of the array (the first empty space in the bottom level of the tree). This new value might be larger than its parent, which would break the heap property, so you need to push this node up the tree until it is no longer larger than its parent and the heap property is restored. More formally, if the new value is larger than the value of its parent node, you bubble it up by swapping it with its parent. For example, if we were to add 60 to the preceding heap, we would insert it at the bottom and swap it upward twice, because at both levels it is larger than its parent node.

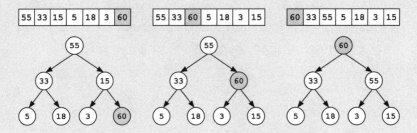

Removal of the max element is similar. The original max value is swapped with the last element of the array, making the last element the new root node.

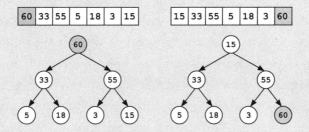

Then the original max value (current last element) is deleted. We have now deleted the correct node, but likely broken the heap property in the process.

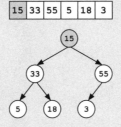

continued

Starting at the new root node, we walk that node down the tree in order to restore the heap property. At each level we compare that node's value to both its children. If it is smaller than either of its children, we move the new root node downward to restore the heap property by swapping places with the larger of its two children. The downward swaps terminate when there are no larger children.

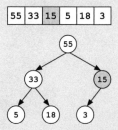

Both insertion of new elements and deletion of the maximum element require us to walk at most one path between the top and bottom of the tree. Since we can approximately double the number of nodes in a heap while adding only a single level of new nodes to the bottom, the operations can be fast even for large heaps. Specifically, we can double the number of nodes and add only one additional step to both of these operations! Furthermore, both operations guarantee that the tree remains balanced, so future operations will be efficient.

Difficult Search Problems

G et out," repeated Dr. Loop.

"I'm here on official police business," Frank responded, not moving from his chair. He could hear soft footsteps behind him as whoever held the crossbow moved forward.

"Unlikely," said Dr. Loop. "I've known Captain Donovan a long time, and he's not the sort to rely on private investigators. As I recall, he takes particular pleasure in developing novel threats to keep busybodies away from active cases."

Frank started to reach into his pocket.

"No sudden moves," said a gruff voice behind him.

Frank felt his temper flare. He hated having crossbows pointed at him, an admittedly common experience in his profession. "I'm getting a parchment," he said through gritted teeth.

"Get it slowly then," said the voice. "If you move quickly, I *will* shoot."

Frank groaned silently. Only one type of person spoke like that— Booleans. Booleans' black-and-white view of the world made them particularly effective as security guards. You couldn't talk yourself out of trouble with a Boolean. Either you were breaking the rules, or you weren't.

Frank moved extra slowly as he retrieved the captain's letter. He leaned forward, taking a full minute to place the letter on the desk. He didn't sit back. The less he moved, the better.

After studying the note for a while, Dr. Loop nodded to her guard. Frank heard the crossbow's safety snap on. He exhaled in relief and leaned back in the chair. Dr. Loop waved the guard out of the room.

"You had Captain Donovan write you a letter of introduction?" asked Dr. Loop.

"As you said, it's a sensitive topic," replied Frank.

"And you probably heard of my reputation." Dr. Loop chuckled.

"*I took your class*," Frank muttered, but Dr. Loop didn't hear.

"So you're investigating the thefts. What do you want to know?"

In an instant her demeanor had changed completely. Her eyes rapidly scanned his face, as though analyzing every reaction. All traces of pleasantry were gone; her voice was all business. Frank wondered how much of her pleasant chit-chat had been an act. Wizard Criminology was a dangerous field, and Dr. Loop had survived a long time.

"What magical protections do police stations have?" asked Frank.

"Basic alerting spells," said Dr. Loop. "They will tell you if someone uses magic in the station, but they won't prevent it."

"Why not a magical barrier?"

"Not practical," explained the professor. "The police force uses too many wizard consultants. They need to be able to cast divining spells on the evidence, truth spells for the prisoners, magical mirroring spells for the records, and reheating spells for lunch."

Frank nodded, remembering the conversation about magical priority queues.

"It would be too expensive anyway," added Dr. Loop. "Only the royal castle and prison have more than the basic alerting spells. The castle has a bunch of protection spells, but no dampening spells. Marcus does too much work there for the king."

"So someone could use magic in the castle?" Frank confirmed.

"They could," replied Dr. Loop, "but it wouldn't be wise. The castle has a dozen protective spells that will block offensive magic. King Fredrick also employs a half-dozen wizard guards. They're junior, but they can undo a basic curse. And then there is Marcus. Few wizards would want to cross him."

"What about artifacts?"

"Ah. Now that's a good question. It depends on the artifact. The castle has protection against weaponized artifacts, of course, but nothing can protect against all artifacts. There are simply too many varieties. Since most artifacts don't require new magic (having been previously enchanted), not even the spell-blocking spells in the prison could help there."

"What?" asked Frank. "I thought the prison was immune to all magic. Don't they keep evil wizards there? In fact, isn't Exponentious there? He tried to destroy the entire kingdom with magic. Why don't they just block all magical artifacts from working?"

Dr. Loop gave a dry laugh. "Sorry to disappoint you, but you can't block all the artifacts. Don't worry, though; the royal wizards keep the most powerful ones well guarded. And all prisoners are thoroughly searched when they arrive."

"What other protection does the prison have?" asked Frank, panic building as the pieces started to fall into place.

"Let's see," said Dr. Loop. She began to tick off the list on her fingers. "Stone walls, a moat filled with cranky badgers, a hundred guards, heavy oak doors, a few ornamental pine doors, the Spell of Mild Nausea in each hallway, the Spell of Difficult Searching, the—"

"Spell of Difficult Searching?" interrupted Frank.

"It isn't new," Dr. Loop explained. "They cast a load of protective spells on the prison before they cast the Spell of Spell Blocking."

"What does the Spell of Difficult Searching do?" asked Frank, a feeling of dread rising in his chest.

"Makes it hard to find a prisoner's cell. More accurately, it magically swaps cells. If you picture the cells as a giant array, the Spell of Difficult Searching would be an algorithm that swaps array indexes. It does a random swap of everything at midnight each night.

"It makes it hard for anyone to break out their friends. Without structure in the array values, intruders have to rely on exhaustive search. And, since the cells are shuffled daily, you can't break up the search over several nights. The guards complain that the randomness is just annoying. They spend hours each day taking roll call. Although I heard that they've recently made a game around it called 'Who's Behind the Next Door?' Bets can get up to a silver piece per door."

"Do they write down the new cell locations?"

"That would defeat the entire purpose! If they kept a mapping of prisoners to cells, like an inverted index, then you could just look up the prisoner. What good would the spell be if you could break into the capital police station's record room and steal the cell assignments? The goal is to make intruders spend hours searching through the prison, which would clearly be impossible. All the guards know each other."

Frank saw the final piece fall into place. The captain had said that the League of Unnecessary Complexity were followers or accomplices of that evil wizard Exponentious—the most dangerous criminal in the royal prison. Everyone was worried that the league was planning to strike again, maybe even to attack the castle. But the plan was so much simpler than that. The league was planning a prison break; they were going to free their leader. He leapt from his chair, grateful the crossbow-wielding Boolean was no longer behind him, and sprinted for the door.

"Thanks," he called over his shoulder as he started down the stairs.

By the time Frank found Notation, he was breathing hard and had an epic stitch in his side. He managed to gasp out little more than "need your help . . . prison break . . . tonight . . . wizards."

Notation watched him for five minutes with a mixture of concern, interest, and mild annoyance. "Spit it out, Frank," she finally said.

Frank, still bent in half with his hands on his knees, shot her a warning look.

"You were the one who came running down here," she countered. "I believe I heard you wheeze out something about needing my help."

Frank ignored the comment. "I figured it out," he finally managed. "The wizards are going to break into the prison tonight."

Notation looked surprised. "The prison? What does Socks want at the prison?"

"Wait. How did you know about Socks?" Frank asked, caught off guard.

Notation gave Frank a confused look. "What do you mean? I thought you suspected him for a while. Didn't you? He wasn't exactly being subtle."

"Yeah. There were clues," Frank hedged.

Notation fell silent and stared at the ground as the gears in her mind spun at frightening speed, connecting the remaining dots. Suddenly her expression darkened and she looked back at Frank. "Why are you telling me this?" she asked. "I'm off the case, remember?"

Frank stared at her in disbelief. "How could you let something like that stop you?" he asked. "Don't you want to capture the thieves?"

"Of course I do," said Notation sharply. "But the captain said—"

"Forget the captain," interrupted Frank. "This is your case, whether he says so or not. Isn't it?"

Notation looked conflicted, and Frank took the opening.

"Listen," he added, "I need help to get the thieves, and I can't call in the force on this one. At least not yet. I'm pretty sure one of the crooks is impersonating a police officer, but I don't know which one. Until I figure that out, I can't trust anyone."

"Then why trust me?" asked Notation.

"Because you're here," said Frank.

"That's not a good reason," said Notation, clearly offended by the implication.

"Not like that," said Frank, waving off her objections. "I mean because you're at this shop, buying an overpriced heap with your own funds. You obviously care about your job. More importantly, if you were in any way involved with a wizard's prison break, you would simply have the league of evil wizards make you a magic heap. No one in their right mind would walk all the way to the Orb district if they had better options."

Notation stood glaring at Frank. He stepped back as her expression passed through "really angry" and approached "you've made a horrible mistake."

"You *told* me to come here," she said through gritted teeth.

"Good thing, too," said Frank. "I knew exactly where to find you. It was the world's easiest search problem—like finding a value in an array when you know the index. I just came straight to Heaperous's shop. I did have to run, though," he conceded. "I figured you'd be here early, and I didn't want to miss you."

Notation didn't seem relieved. "You sent me here to test whether I was in on the plot?"

"No, I sent you here to get you out of the way," admitted Frank. "The test only occurred to me as I was running here. I thought—"

"You didn't trust me?" asked Notation, her voice cold. Each word sounded like a separate accusation.

"Don't take it personally," said Frank. "I don't trust anyone."

"You . . . you . . . " Notation spluttered, turning progressively deeper shades of red and apparently unable to complete the insult.

After a few minutes had passed, Frank asked, "Are you in?"

She nodded stiffly.

"Good," said Frank. "Meet me at the prison in two hours and bring a crossbow."

Notation nodded again.

"And a bowl," Frank added.

"A bowl?" Notation asked, momentarily surprised out of her anger.

Frank flashed a broad smile. "There's some Spell of Mild Nausea in the prison corridors. You might need someplace to vomit."

POLICE ALGORITHMS 101:
FINAL EXAM REVIEW SESSION
Excerpt from Professor Drecker's Lecture

If you learned only one thing from this class, it should be that *the key to efficient algorithms is information.* When approaching a new problem, take the time to understand the structure of the problem and its data. The more structure the problem has, the more potential you have to utilize this information. As you've seen, finding a value in a sorted array is significantly easier than in a completely random array. Sometime you can even build auxiliary data structures, such as heaps or inverted indexes, to provide the structure you need. Regardless, your first step should always be to understand the problem.

Search Termination

At 12:01 AM, the door squeaked open and a guard poked his head into the dark prison cell. He scanned the room slowly with a torch, until his gaze landed on the sleeping prisoner.

"Master?" called the guard softly.

The prisoner stirred, sat up, and looked at the guard.

"Master, I—" started the guard, but he broke off with a strangled gasp.

Frank waved at him from the prison bed.

The guard turned to run, but Notation stepped into the doorway holding a large crossbow.

"I . . . I was just doing my rounds," said the guard.

Frank grunted a laugh and shook his head. "Hand over the torch. Slowly," he instructed. "My friend here just graduated from the police academy, and I'm told she scored top marks in crossbow usage."

"I was second, actually," said Notation from the doorway.

Frank sighed. "Really? This is the one time you decide to be modest?"

"Sorry. I just wanted to be accurate."

"It's a threat, Notation. You're allowed to embellish threats."

"Sorry," she repeated.

"Anyway, the point remains. She has a crossbow and knows how to use it better than all but one of her classmates. Please hand over the torch."

The guard's eyes darted around the room, searching for an escape. Finding none, he slowly leaned forward and offered the torch to Frank. As Frank reached for it, the guard shifted and swung it at his head. The fire hissed through the air.

Frank leaned left to avoid the flaming tip. The guard pivoted for another swing, but Frank stood and plucked the torch from his hands as Notation shoved the guard from behind. He stumbled and fell in an awkward heap on the bed.

Frank shook his head. "Obvious move, kid," he said. "Trying to hit me with a torch. Awful execution. Didn't even come close. I'll give you credit for trying, though."

The guard blinked dumbly back at Frank.

"Now take off that stupid mask. We know it's you, Socks."

"Socks? Who is that? I've never heard of anyone named Socks," said the guard, completely unconvincingly.

"Socks, take off the mask," repeated Frank.

The guard hesitated for a moment before reaching behind his neck and undoing a clasp. A strange whirling sound filled the cell as his face melted and reformed into an elaborate mask. The guard then lowered the mask from his face to reveal Socks.

"How did you know?" asked Socks.

"Many little things," said Frank. "First, you followed us, but didn't reveal yourself until the Vinettees had us cornered. They have a fierce reputation

but aren't the most clever gang when it comes to gloating to their prisoners. They posed the real threat of accidentally revealing your plans. But your story was pathetic enough to be believable.

"Your actions on Frayed Cable Island were less believable, though. It was your dropped staff that destroyed the evidence. You appeared stymied by the gate outside the prison, but immediately seized upon a metal-weakening spell when your own life was in danger. You even used the Spell of Accelerated Rusting, the very same spell that was used during the attack on the convoy."

"You also refused to help pick the lock outside the prison until I suggested climbing over it alone," added Notation. "I'm guessing you wanted to be there if we found the papers."

"Why not confront me then?" asked Socks.

"I still wasn't sure who to trust," admitted Frank. He gestured toward Notation, who still stood at the door holding the crossbow. "Notation caught on a little faster. She told me that she started to suspect you after the prison, but didn't have anything solid. When I suggested the parallelized search, it prevented her from keeping tabs on you."

"I honestly thought Frank suggested the parallelized search to get you out of the way for a while," Notation admitted.

Frank decided never to mention that the goal had been to get them *both* out of his way. At that point, he had been more suspicious of Notation than of Socks. He'd suggested the parallelized search so he could follow up on the threads alone.

"I have to admit," continued Frank, "your acting during the whole prison episode was pretty good. I actually thought someone had jumped you. At the time, it bothered me that the attacker hadn't stuck around, but I ignored my gut. I should have seen it sooner.

"One thing I don't understand, though, is why you closed the door. Why not just 'trip' and drop your staff?"

Socks shrugged. "The door was an accident. I didn't mean to lock us in. My sleeve got caught on the door as I pretended to trip."

"You played it off well, though," said Frank. "And trapping us certainly helped sell the attack story."

Socks shrugged, but pride flashed across his face.

"But most of all, it was your shortcuts with the binary search tree," said Frank. "Anyone who studies binary search trees knows enough to start at the root when inserting nodes. Your mistake meant that either you weren't the expert you claimed to be or you were trying to sabotage the tree."

Socks smiled. "Not bad," he said. "I thought my incompetent wizard act would be enough to throw you off."

"You were good," conceded Frank. "Good enough to make me repeatedly overlook the obvious."

"Thank you," said Socks. "I did a few seasons of Babbageville community theater back at school."

"It shows," said Frank. "I'm guessing that's why you were the one chosen to impersonate the new transfer when you robbed the record offices. Although I have to admit, I never figured out exactly whom you had chosen to impersonate."

"I used whomever suited the task. There were so many new transfers to choose from."

Frank nodded. It made sense. "Too bad the station doesn't keep records of prison cell assignments. I'm guessing you cleared the shelves that could have contained anything about assignments, cell assignments, Exponentious, notices, prison, prisoners, and room assignments. You stole all those documents for nothing."

"It was worth a try," said Socks. "There's a lot of cells here. But how did you know I was going after the prison? I didn't even mention it."

Frank smiled. "You weren't subtle in your tip about an attack on the castle," he explained. "You were trying to draw security away from the prison—not a bad plan. I might have missed the prison option if I hadn't chatted with Dr. Loop."

Socks scowled at the mention of Dr. Loop's name. "Her? She's been a thorn in the side of evil wizards for years. Do you know that she helped Marcus design the prison's security? Who puts a Spell of Mild Nausea in the hallways? That's just mean."

"It doesn't seem so bad," Notation chimed in. "They give the guards antinausea charms, and the prisoners are safe as long as they're with the guards or in their rooms."

"I threw up twice already," countered Socks.

"You were breaking in! That's why—" started Notation.

Frank cut in, "Where are your accomplices, Socks?"

"He's alone," said Notation before Socks could answer.

"What?" Frank looked at her. "How do you know that?"

"There's another six-pen ArrayCart parked outside," she answered. "I have no idea why he would use the same cart, but it's out there and it's empty. If he was working with others, someone would be guarding it or waiting to make a getaway."

Socks shrugged. "Only one of us could use the mask to sneak into the prison itself, and large groups hanging around outside a prison are generally considered suspicious. So I volunteered to come alone."

"Where can I find your friends?" asked Frank.

Socks laughed. "You won't need to find *them*, Mr. Runtime. Once news of my capture gets out, they'll find *you*. You've made some powerful enemies tonight."

"Oh, really?" said Frank. "I seem to be good at making enemies. Perhaps you can give me their names, and I can add them to my fan club. Is Gretchen in on it too?"

Socks laughed. "Gretchen? You actually still think I'm her apprentice? After you two revealed all the other lies?"

"Then who's behind this?" asked Notation.

"The League of Unnecessary Complexity," answered Frank. Mentally he added, "which apparently does not include a wizard named Gretchen."

"I'm impressed, Mr. Runtime," said Socks. "Not many people know about our little organization."

"The League of Unnecessary Complexity?" asked Notation.

"They're involved with the wizard Exponentious: followers, accomplices, or maybe just admirers," Frank explained.

"Exponentious!" exclaimed Notation. "The evil wizard? Isn't he in prison for trying to destroy the *whole kingdom?*"

"Yeah, that's him—the really bad wizard. Didn't I mention he was the one Socks was going to rescue?" asked Frank.

Notation glared back at him.

"You misunderstand," said Socks. "The kingdom wouldn't be in ruins. It would have been saved. Once Exponentious comes to power, we'll witness a new golden age. He—"

"He's insane," interrupted Frank. "He would have ruined the kingdom."

Off to the side Notation nodded in agreement. "I have to agree with Frank on this one."

Socks's eyes shone with fury. He jumped to his feet, flinging back his cloak. He swung up his staff and began chanting a long incantation, whirling the staff in a complex pattern. Socks pointed the staff directly at Frank and finished the spell.

Frank watched calmly as absolutely nothing happened. Notation rolled her eyes.

"Done now?" Frank asked. "You have to know magic doesn't work in here."

"Yeah. I just—" Socks started, slumped in defeat. He broke off suddenly and bolted for the door. Before Notation could fire, Socks swung his staff at the crossbow. She stepped out of range and repositioned the crossbow, mildly disappointed at the pathetic escape attempt. At the same time, Frank grabbed the back of Socks's robe and pulled him to a stop. The kid's arms windmilled as he fought to break free.

With a grunt, Frank heaved on the robe and Socks stumbled back into the cell, toppling onto the bed. Frank crouched to retrieve the fallen staff. It was useless for magic, but could still raise a nasty welt. Then he strode out. As soon as he was clear, Notation slammed the door.

Epilogue

Notation was waiting in the hall when Frank emerged from the captain's office. "How'd it go?" she asked the moment he shut the door.

"Well enough," said Frank. "He didn't yell, and I've got another three months' rent for my office." He held up a small bag of coins.

"That's it?" asked Notation, her voice laced with disappointment.

"What were you expecting?" asked Frank. "A commendation? They don't give commendations to private eyes. But I hear you got one, and a promotion. Well done, Detective Notation. It's quite a step up."

Notation blushed. "Thank you," she said. "But what about you? I thought . . . maybe . . ."

"You thought the captain would ask me to come back," Frank filled in. "In fact, he tells me you recommended it."

Notation turned a bright shade of red. "You're a skilled detective," she said.

Frank laughed. "He didn't offer me a job." Seeing the look on Notation's face, he added, "Don't take it personally. He was never going to offer me a spot on the force again. The captain and I have a long history, longer than a single case can erase. Anyway, the private eye life suits me better."

"So you just go back to . . ."

"Hunting someone's lost dragon?"

"Yeah," said Notation. "That."

"As a matter of fact, I've been presented with a new opportunity." He held up his hand to stop her before she could get too excited, and added, "As an independent contractor."

"What is it?" asked Notation.

"It appears there's a league of wizards out there, trying to free Exponentious and take over the kingdom."

Notation smiled. "I'm familiar with them. I seem to recall that I recently helped arrest one of their more active members."

"One of their more active members, yes, and dedicated members, for sure. But it's possible that he was also one of the less capable members. Princess Ann is concerned that Socks's attempted prison break will inspire some of the league's more senior and competent members."

"So you're investigating the League of Unnecessary Complexity? As an independent contractor, of course."

Frank nodded. "It's a tough search problem—find all the members of a secret evil organization. But it just so happens that search problems are my specialty."

Index

intersection, 130
inverted indexes,
129–133, 226
iterative deepening, 118–126
on graphs, 125–126
on grids, 120–123

K

Kingdom Highway Map,
78, 91

L

last-in, first-out data structures, 95–96, 99. *See
also* stacks
League of Magical
Confectioners, 151
linear search, 15–16
locks,
and best-first search,
203–205
and breadth-first search,
72–77
and priority queues,
203–205

M

Manhattan distance, 191

N

nodes
child, 138, 143
graph, 78, 91, 136
inserting
in binary search tree,
167–169
in heap, 220–221

root
of binary search tree,
138, 143
of heap, 220
tree, 73, 138, 143–144

P

parallel algorithms, 110–112,
115–116
prefix trees, 177–182
priority queues, 194–197,
199–200
and best-first search, 196,
203–205
dequeue, 195
enqueue, 195
and heaps, 219
for investigations, 194–197
for locks, 203–205

Q

queues, 77, 96–97, 195. *See
also* priority queues
and arrays, 100–101
and breadth-first search, 107
dequeue, 97, 100–101
enqueue, 97, 100

R

range search, 153–162
recursive algorithms, 155
for binary search tree construction, 147–150
for range search, 153–162
root node
of binary search tree,
138, 143
of heap, 220

UPDATES

Visit *https://www.nostarch.com/searchtale/* for updates, errata, and other information.

More no-nonsense books from **no starch press**

THE MANGA GUIDE TO DATABASES

by MANA TAKAHASHI, SHOKO AZUMA, *and* TREND-PRO CO., LTD.
JAN 2009, 224 PP., $19.95
ISBN 978-1-59327-190-9

INVENT YOUR OWN COMPUTER GAMES WITH PYTHON

by AL SWEIGART
FALL 2016, 368 PP., $29.95
ISBN 978-1-59327-795-6

LAUREN IPSUM
A STORY ABOUT COMPUTER SCIENCE AND OTHER IMPROBABLE THINGS

by CARLOS BUENO
DEC 2014, 192 PP., $16.95
ISBN 978-1-59327-574-7
full color

HOW SOFTWARE WORKS
THE MAGIC BEHIND ENCRYPTION, CGI, SEARCH ENGINES, AND OTHER EVERYDAY TECHNOLOGIES

by V. ANTON SPRAUL
AUG 2015, 216 PP., $29.95
ISBN 978-1-59327-666-9

THINK LIKE A PROGRAMMER
AN INTRODUCTION TO CREATIVE PROBLEM SOLVING

by V. ANTON SPRAUL
AUG 2012, 256 PP., $34.95
ISBN 978-1-59327-424-5

LEARN TO PROGRAM WITH MINECRAFT
TRANSFORM YOUR WORLD WITH THE POWER OF PYTHON

by CRAIG RICHARDSON
DEC 2015, 320 PP., $29.95
ISBN 978-1-59327-670-6
full color

800.420.7240 or 415.863.9900 | sales@nostarch.com | www.nostarch.com